Drawn & Quarterly
SHOWCASE
BOOK TWO

An anthology of new illustrated fiction.

Drawn & Quarterly Showcase; book two of a continuing annual series. Entire contents © copyright 2004 by Pentti Otsamo, Jeffrey Brown, and Erik De Graaf. All rights reserved. No part of this book (except small portions for review purposes) may be reproduced in any form without written permission from the respective cartoonists or Drawn & Quarterly. Editor & publisher: Chris Oliveros. Production: Tom Devlin and Chris Oliveros. Publicity: Peggy Burns.

Drawn & Quarterly
Post Office Box 48056
Montreal, Quebec
Canada H2V 4S8
www.drawnandquarterly.com

Printed in Hong Kong in June 2004.

10 9 8 7 6 5 4 3 2 1
National Library of Canada Cataloguing in Publication
    Drawn & Quarterly Showcase : book 2 : an anthology of new illustrated fiction / Jeffrey Brown, Erik De Graaf, Pentti Otsamo.
ISBN 1-896597-81-5
    1. Comic books, strips, etc. I. Brown, Jeffrey II. Graaf, Erik De III. Otsamo, Pentti IV. Title: Drawn & Quarterly Showcase.
PN6720.D732 2004   741.5'9   C2004-901494-3

Distributed in the USA and abroad by:
Chronicle Books
85 Second Street
San Francisco, CA 94105
800.722.6657

Distributed in Canada by:
Raincoast Books
9050 Shaughnessy Street
Vancouver, BC V6P 6E5
800.663.5714

Covers:

Pentti Otsamo

Endpapers:

Erik De Graaf

Pages 5 to 37:

Pentti Otsamo

Pages 38 to 79:

Jeffrey Brown

Pages 81 to 96:

Erik De Graaf

Pentti Otsamo

Pentti Otsamo was born in 1967 in Oulu, Finland. His first translated short stories appeared in issues of DRAWN & QUARTERLY in the mid 1990s and by 1998 his first graphic novella in English, THE FALL OF HOMUNCULUS, was published.

Of his work, Otsamo writes, "For me, comics are a way of telling stories. It's less satisfying to make a picture, a piece of art, just for art's sake, the story must be dominating. Stories are, of course, often related somehow to my life. I think that's hard to avoid, there's always a connection."

He lives in the Finnish countryside with his wife and three children where he is now working on a weekly comic strip for Helsinki's largest newspaper.

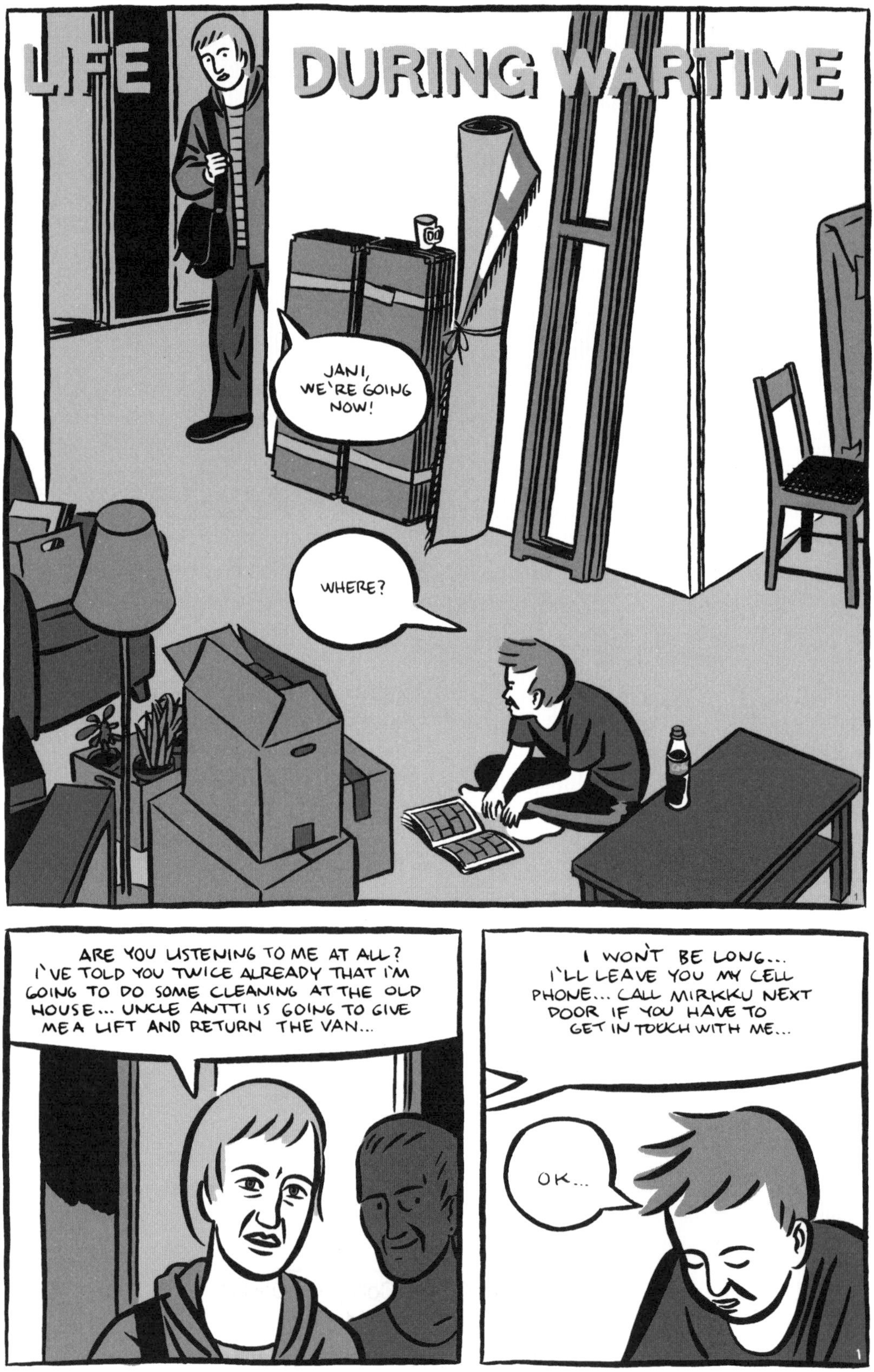
LIFE DURING WARTIME
JANI, WE'RE GOING NOW!
WHERE?
ARE YOU LISTENING TO ME AT ALL? I'VE TOLD YOU TWICE ALREADY THAT I'M GOING TO DO SOME CLEANING AT THE OLD HOUSE... UNCLE ANTTI IS GOING TO GIVE ME A LIFT AND RETURN THE VAN...
I WON'T BE LONG... I'LL LEAVE YOU MY CELL PHONE... CALL MIRKKU NEXT DOOR IF YOU HAVE TO GET IN TOUCH WITH ME...
OK...

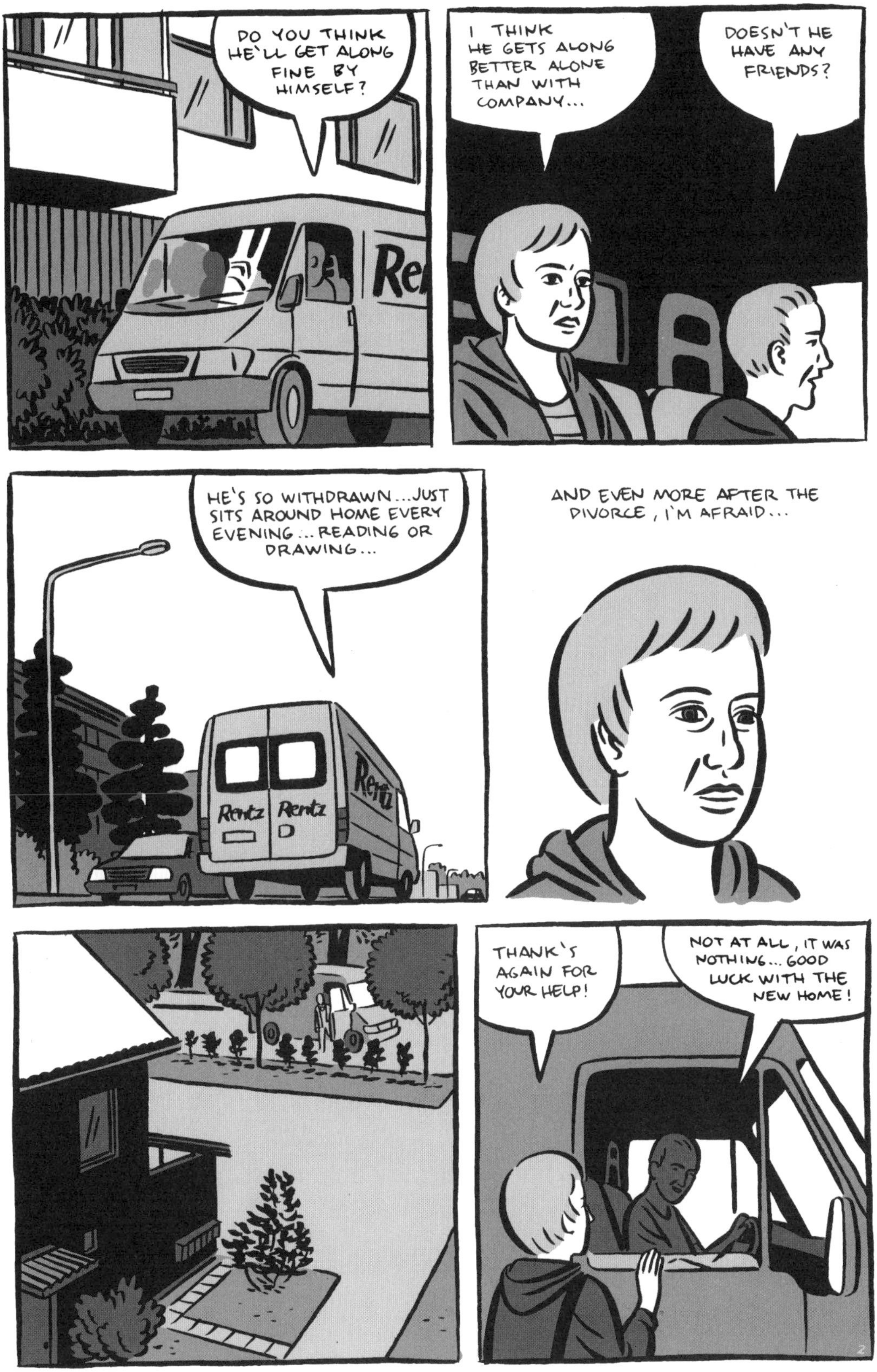

DO YOU THINK HE'LL GET ALONG FINE BY HIMSELF?
Rentz
I THINK HE GETS ALONG BETTER ALONE THAN WITH COMPANY...
DOESN'T HE HAVE ANY FRIENDS?
HE'S SO WITHDRAWN...JUST SITS AROUND HOME EVERY EVENING...READING OR DRAWING...
Rentz Rentz Rentz
AND EVEN MORE AFTER THE DIVORCE, I'M AFRAID...
THANK'S AGAIN FOR YOUR HELP!
NOT AT ALL, IT WAS NOTHING...GOOD LUCK WITH THE NEW HOME!
2

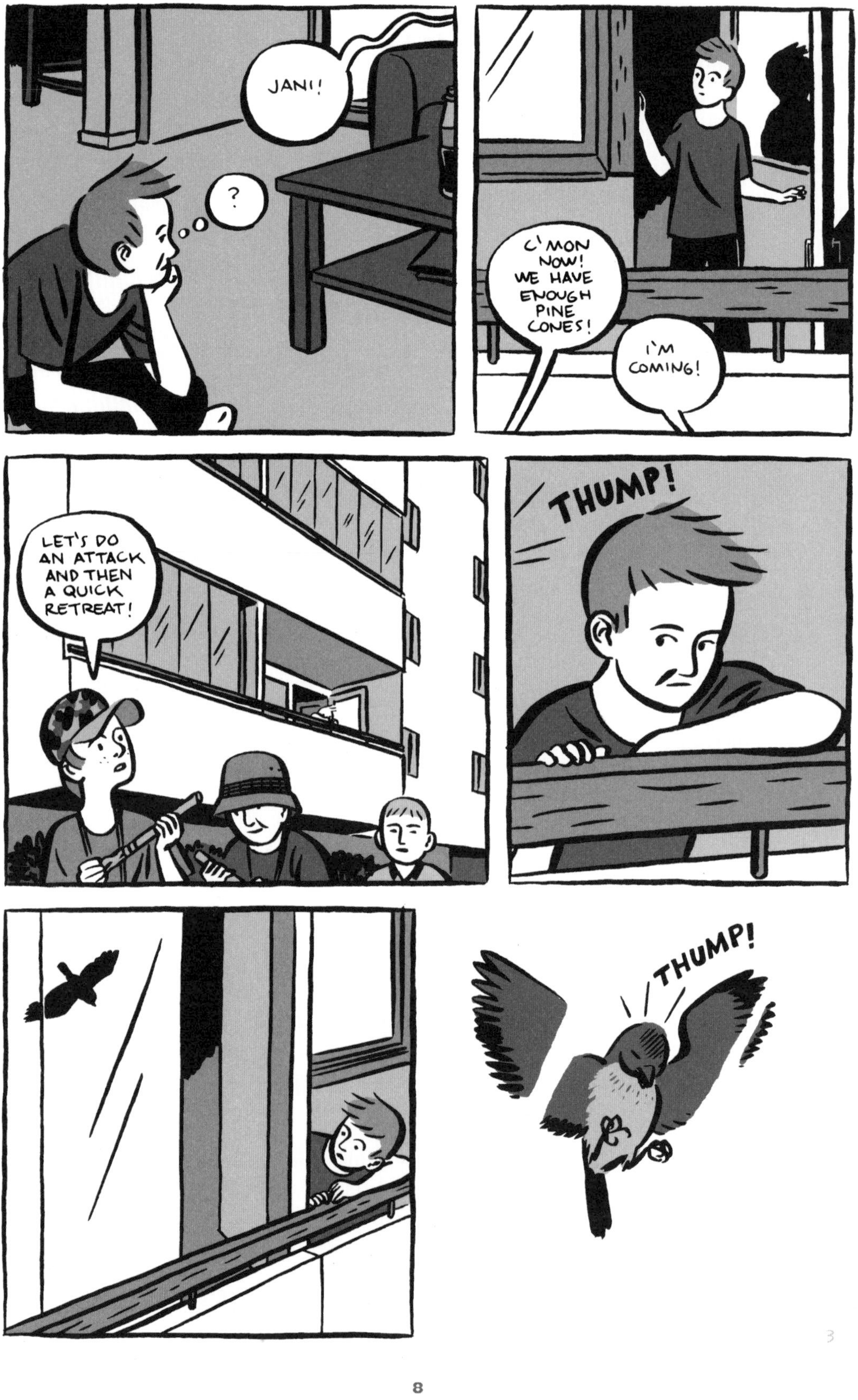
JANI!
?
C'MON NOW! WE HAVE ENOUGH PINE CONES!
I'M COMING!
LET'S DO AN ATTACK AND THEN A QUICK RETREAT!
THUMP!
THUMP!

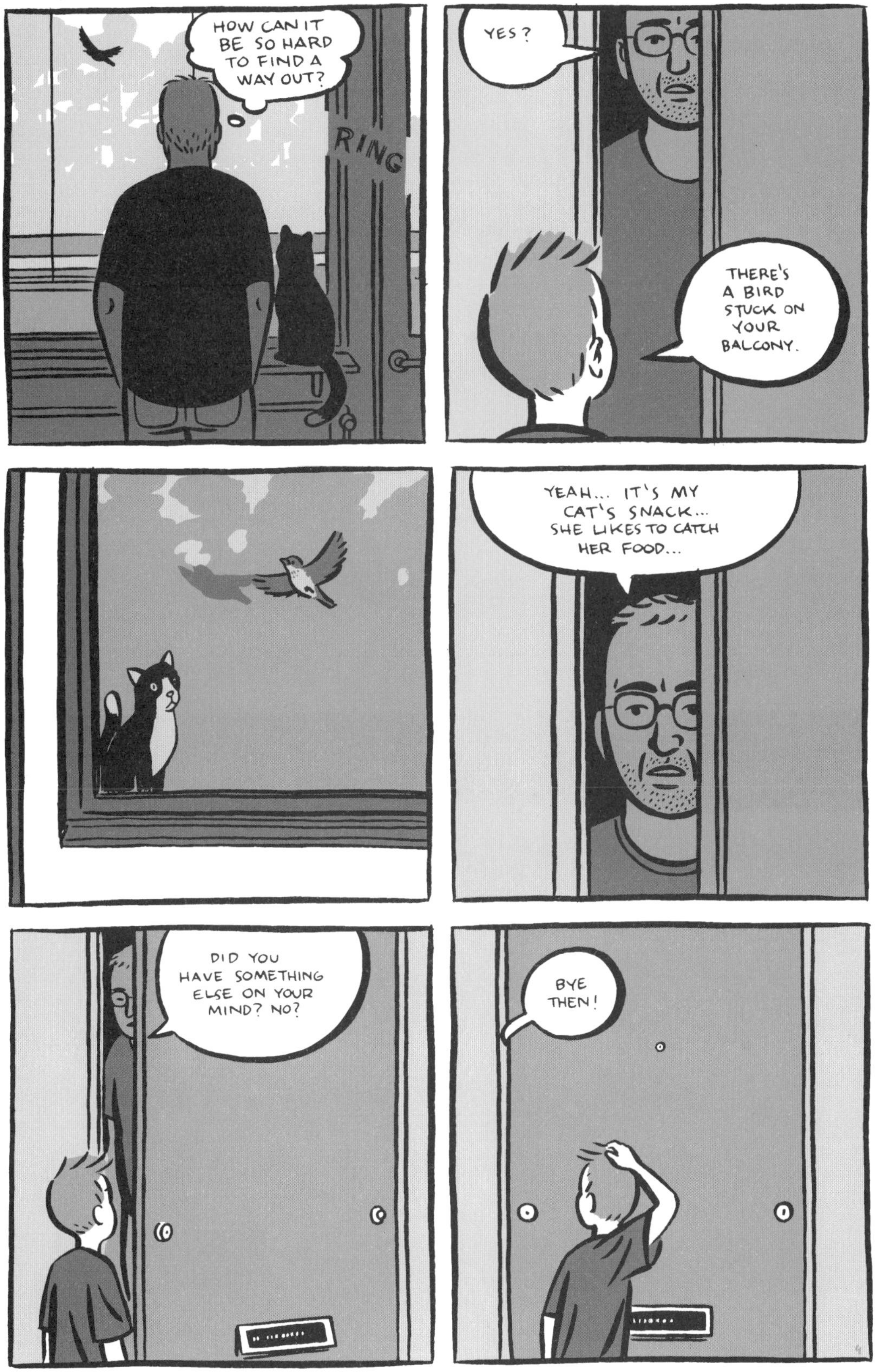
HOW CAN IT BE SO HARD TO FIND A WAY OUT?
RING
YES?
THERE'S A BIRD STUCK ON YOUR BALCONY.
YEAH... IT'S MY CAT'S SNACK... SHE LIKES TO CATCH HER FOOD...
DID YOU HAVE SOMETHING ELSE ON YOUR MIND? NO?
BYE THEN!

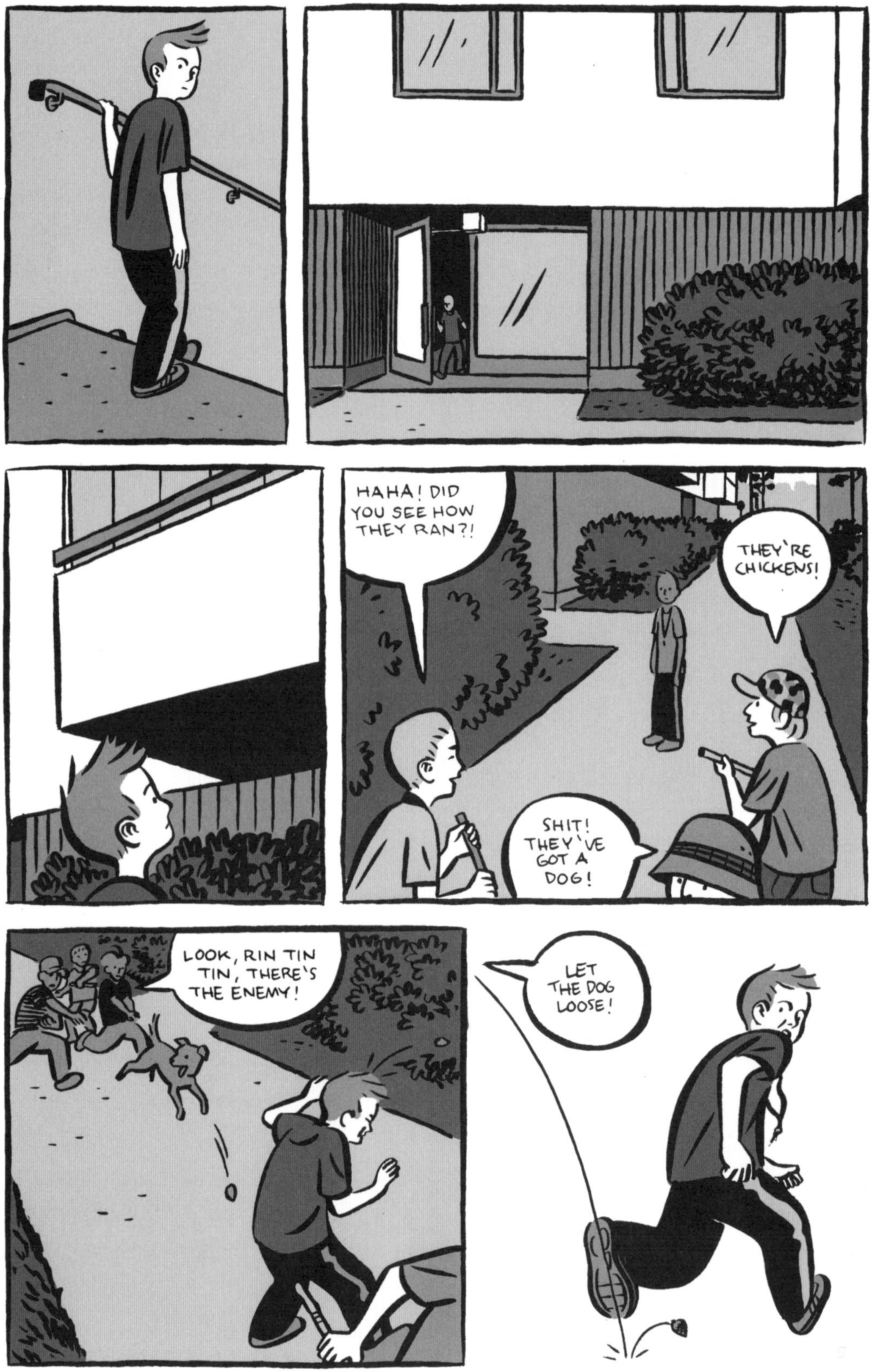
HAHA! DID YOU SEE HOW THEY RAN?!
THEY'RE CHICKENS!
SHIT! THEY'VE GOT A DOG!
LOOK, RIN TIN TIN, THERE'S THE ENEMY!
LET THE DOG LOOSE!

AT HIM, RIN TIN TIN!
THAT DOG NEVER CATCHES ANYTHING!
WELL, ONCE HE ALMOST CAUGHT A CAT...
I THINK THAT 45 DEGREE RULE IS TOTALLY SENSELESS!
WELL, THOSE EROTIC MOVIES ON TV ARE NOTHING TO BOAST ABOUT ANYWAY...
STOP, RIN TIN TIN, STOP!

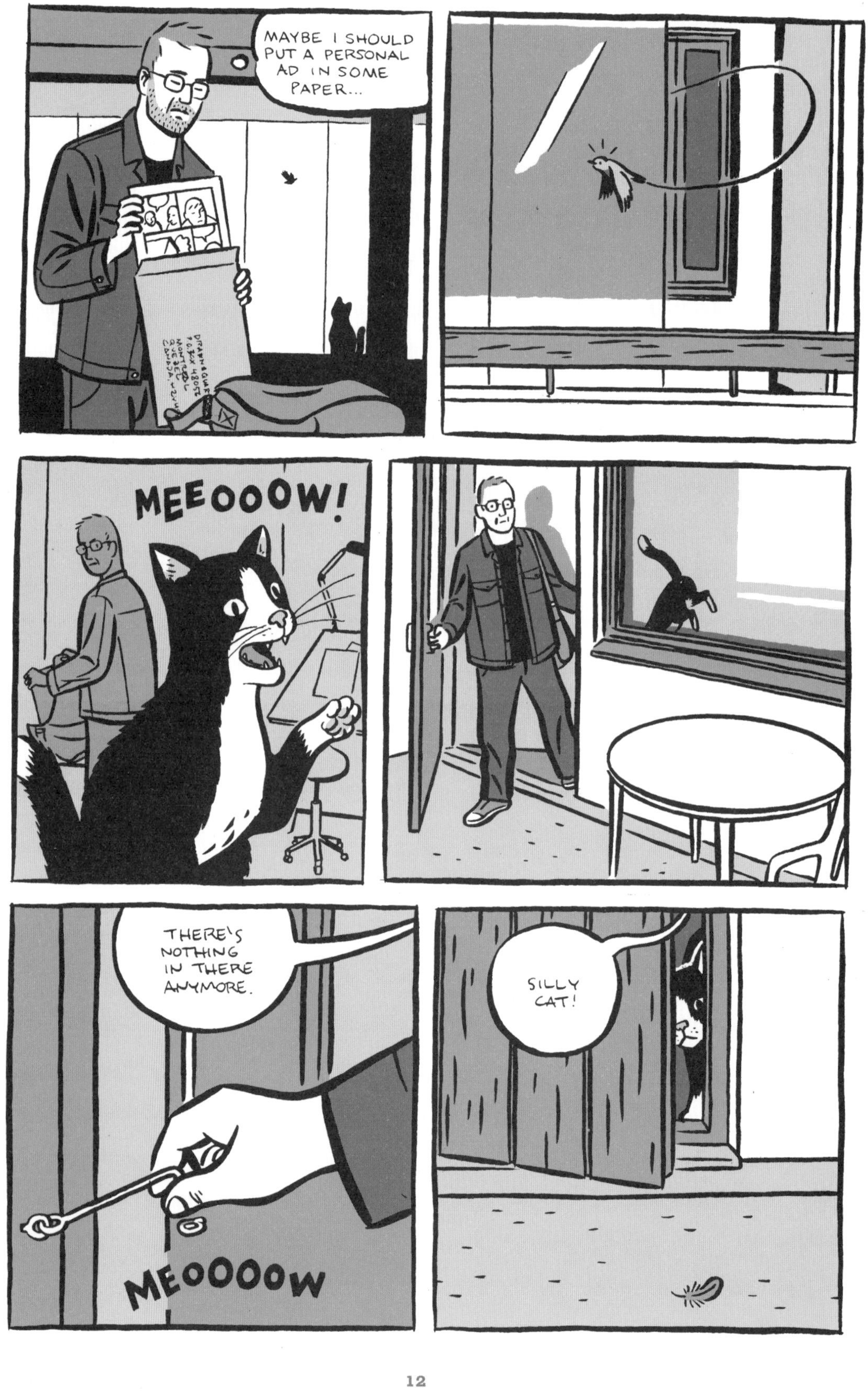
MAYBE I SHOULD PUT A PERSONAL AD IN SOME PAPER...
MEEOOOW!
THERE'S NOTHING IN THERE ANYMORE.
MEOOOOW
SILLY CAT!

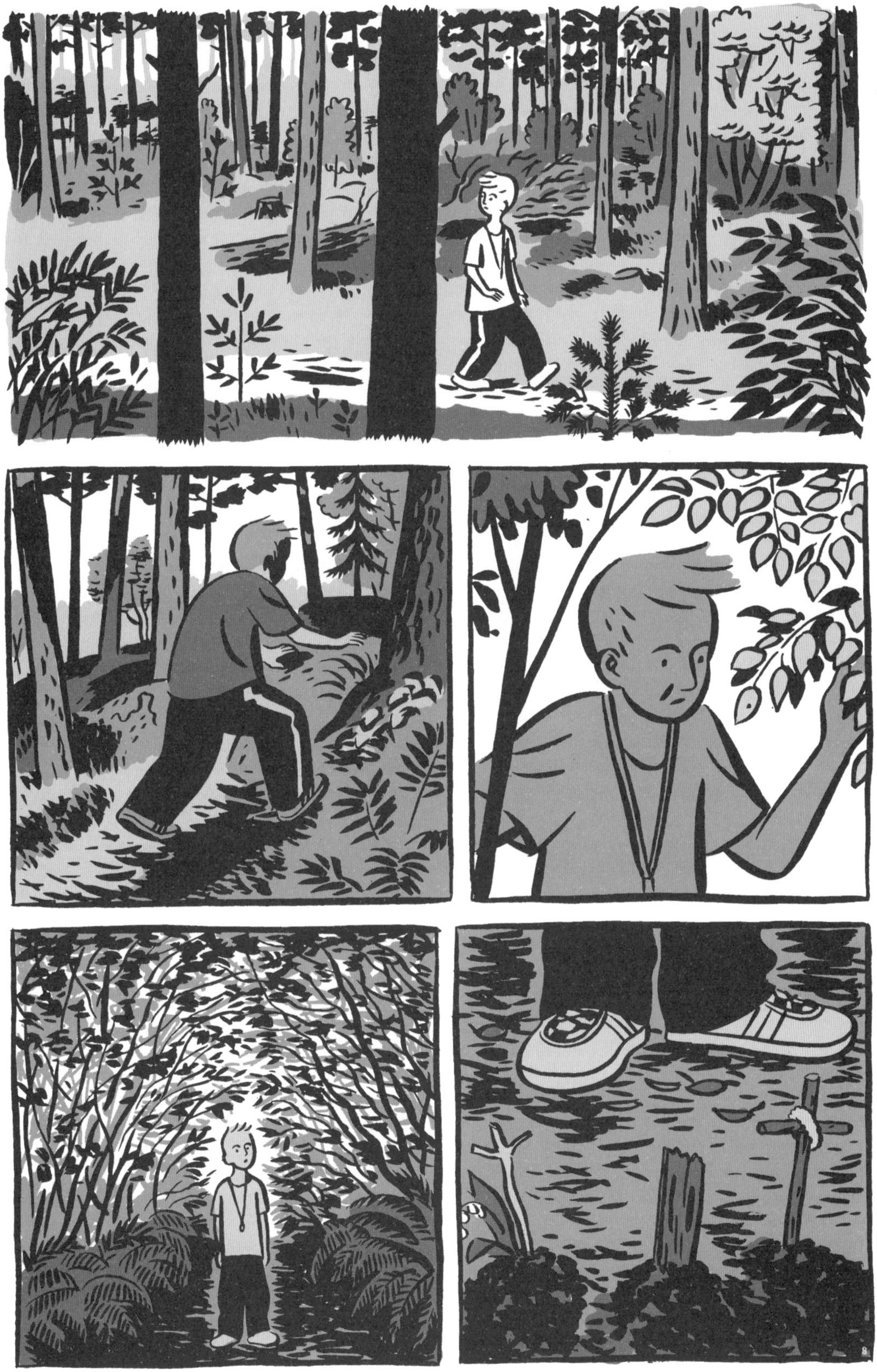

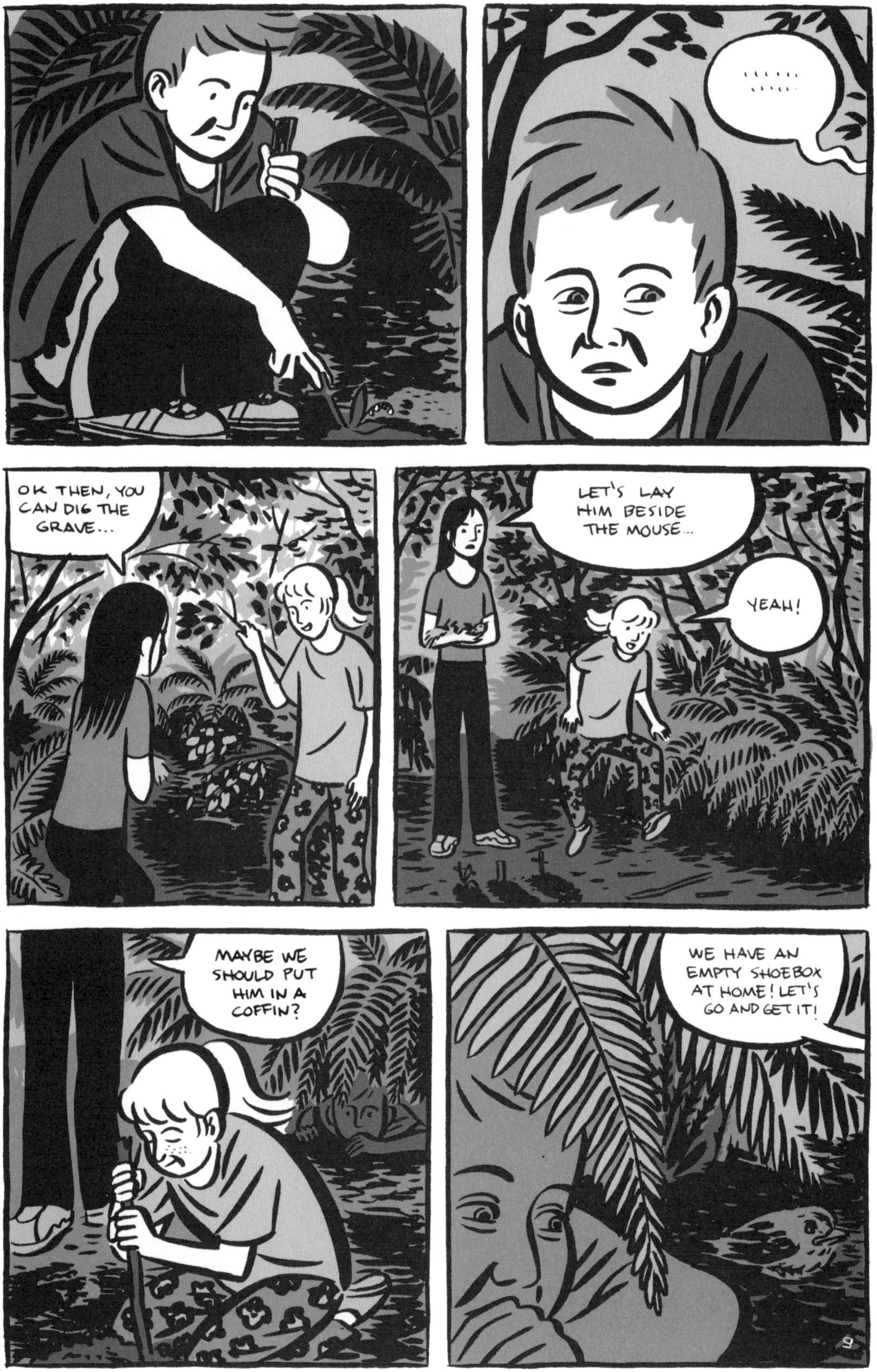
OK THEN, YOU CAN DIG THE GRAVE...
LET'S LAY HIM BESIDE THE MOUSE...
YEAH!
MAYBE WE SHOULD PUT HIM IN A COFFIN?
WE HAVE AN EMPTY SHOEBOX AT HOME! LET'S GO AND GET IT!
9

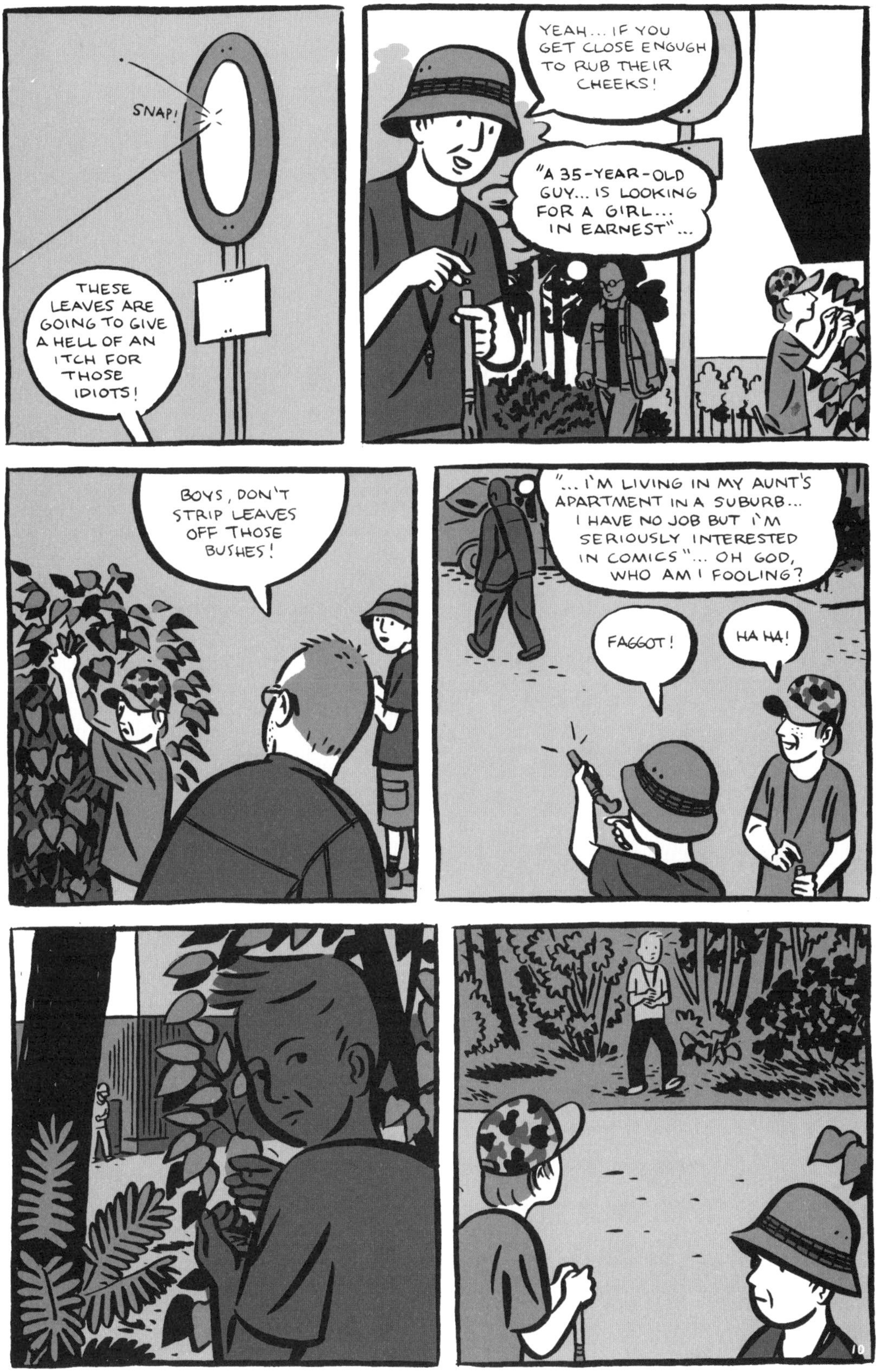

SNAP!
THESE LEAVES ARE GOING TO GIVE A HELL OF AN ITCH FOR THOSE IDIOTS!
YEAH... IF YOU GET CLOSE ENOUGH TO RUB THEIR CHEEKS!
"A 35-YEAR-OLD GUY... IS LOOKING FOR A GIRL... IN EARNEST"...
BOYS, DON'T STRIP LEAVES OFF THOSE BUSHES!
"... I'M LIVING IN MY AUNT'S APARTMENT IN A SUBURB... I HAVE NO JOB BUT I'M SERIOUSLY INTERESTED IN COMICS"... OH GOD, WHO AM I FOOLING?
FAGGOT!
HA HA!
10

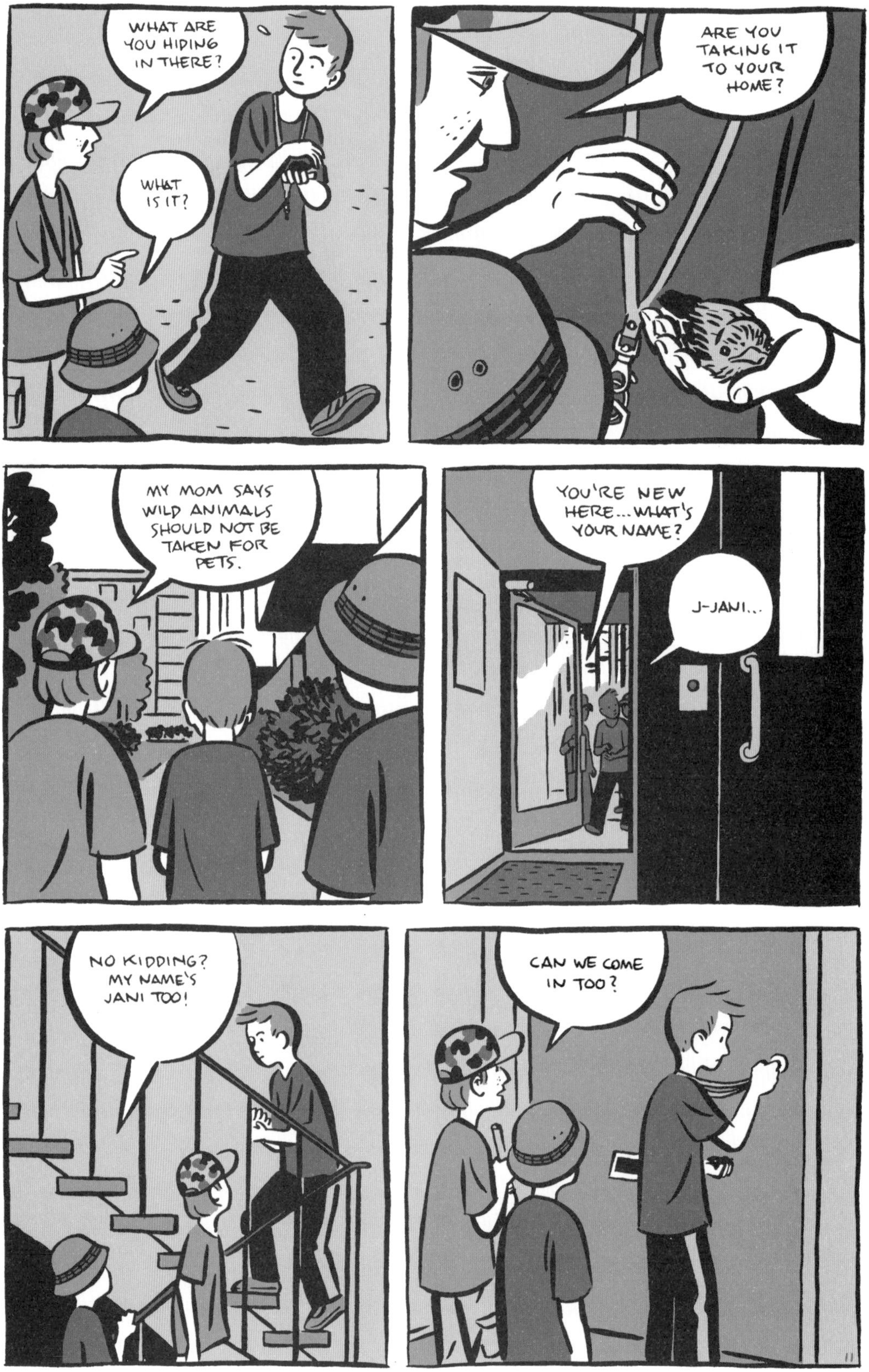
WHAT ARE YOU HIDING IN THERE?
WHAT IS IT?
ARE YOU TAKING IT TO YOUR HOME?
MY MOM SAYS WILD ANIMALS SHOULD NOT BE TAKEN FOR PETS.
YOU'RE NEW HERE... WHAT'S YOUR NAME?
J-JANI...
NO KIDDING? MY NAME'S JANI TOO!
CAN WE COME IN TOO?

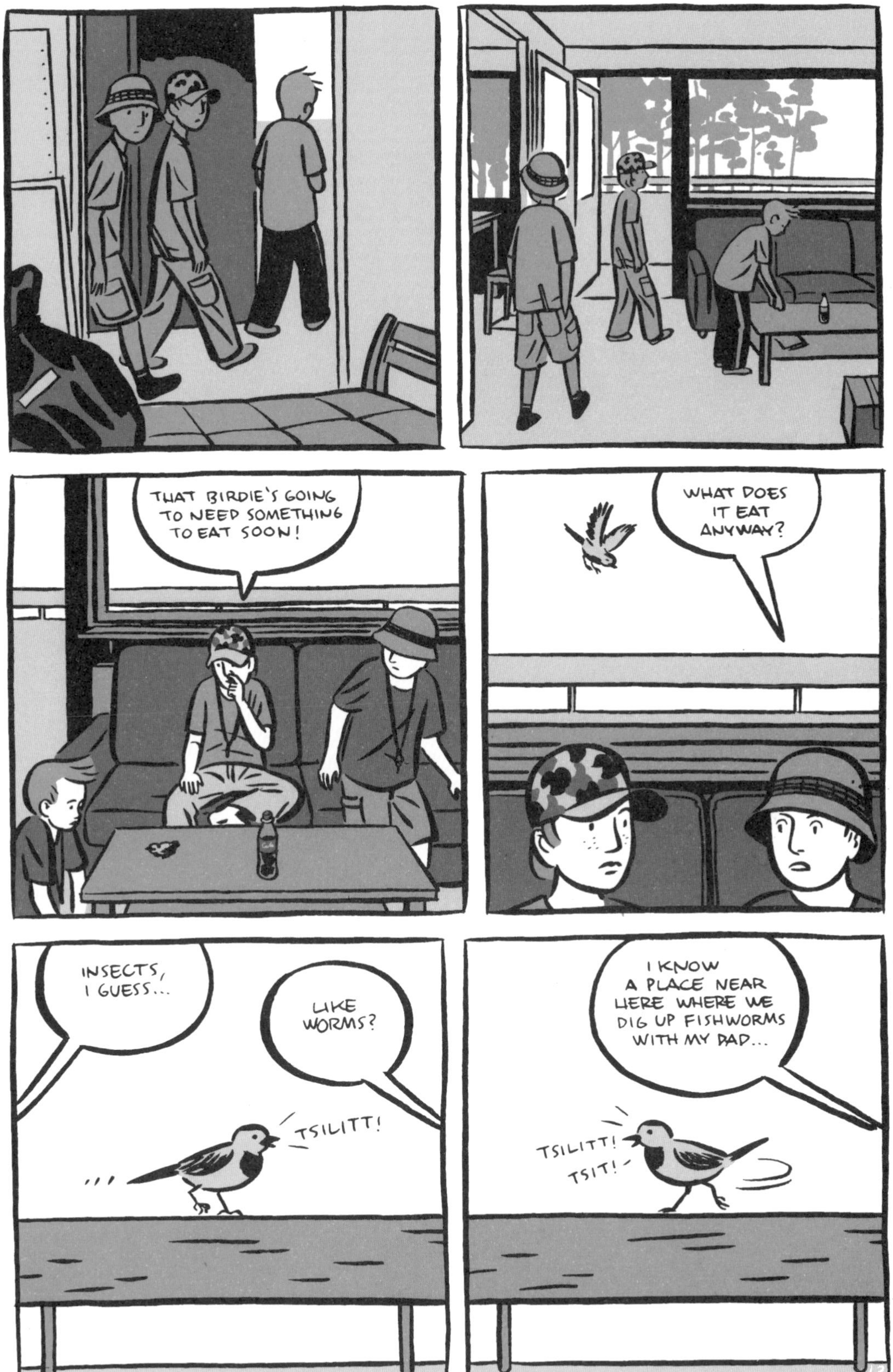
THAT BIRDIE'S GOING TO NEED SOMETHING TO EAT SOON!
WHAT DOES IT EAT ANYWAY?
INSECTS, I GUESS...
LIKE WORMS?
TSILITT!
I KNOW A PLACE NEAR HERE WHERE WE DIG UP FISHWORMS WITH MY DAD...
TSILITT!
TSIT!

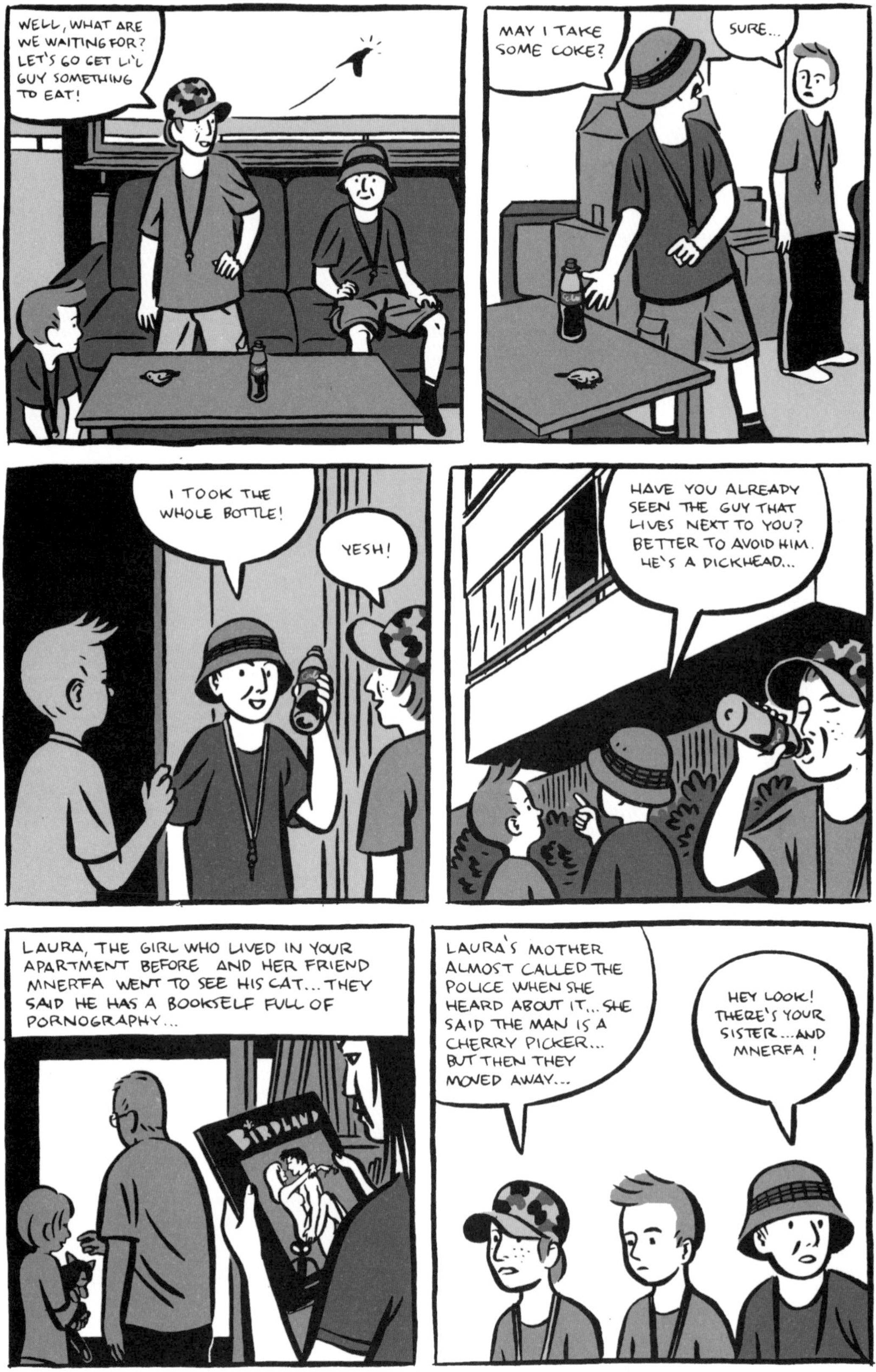
WELL, WHAT ARE WE WAITING FOR? LET'S GO GET LI'L GUY SOMETHING TO EAT!
MAY I TAKE SOME COKE?
SURE...
I TOOK THE WHOLE BOTTLE!
YESH!
HAVE YOU ALREADY SEEN THE GUY THAT LIVES NEXT TO YOU? BETTER TO AVOID HIM. HE'S A DICKHEAD...
LAURA, THE GIRL WHO LIVED IN YOUR APARTMENT BEFORE AND HER FRIEND MNERFA WENT TO SEE HIS CAT... THEY SAID HE HAS A BOOKSELF FULL OF PORNOGRAPHY...
BIRDLAND
LAURA'S MOTHER ALMOST CALLED THE POLICE WHEN SHE HEARD ABOUT IT... SHE SAID THE MAN IS A CHERRY PICKER... BUT THEN THEY MOVED AWAY...
HEY LOOK! THERE'S YOUR SISTER... AND MNERFA!

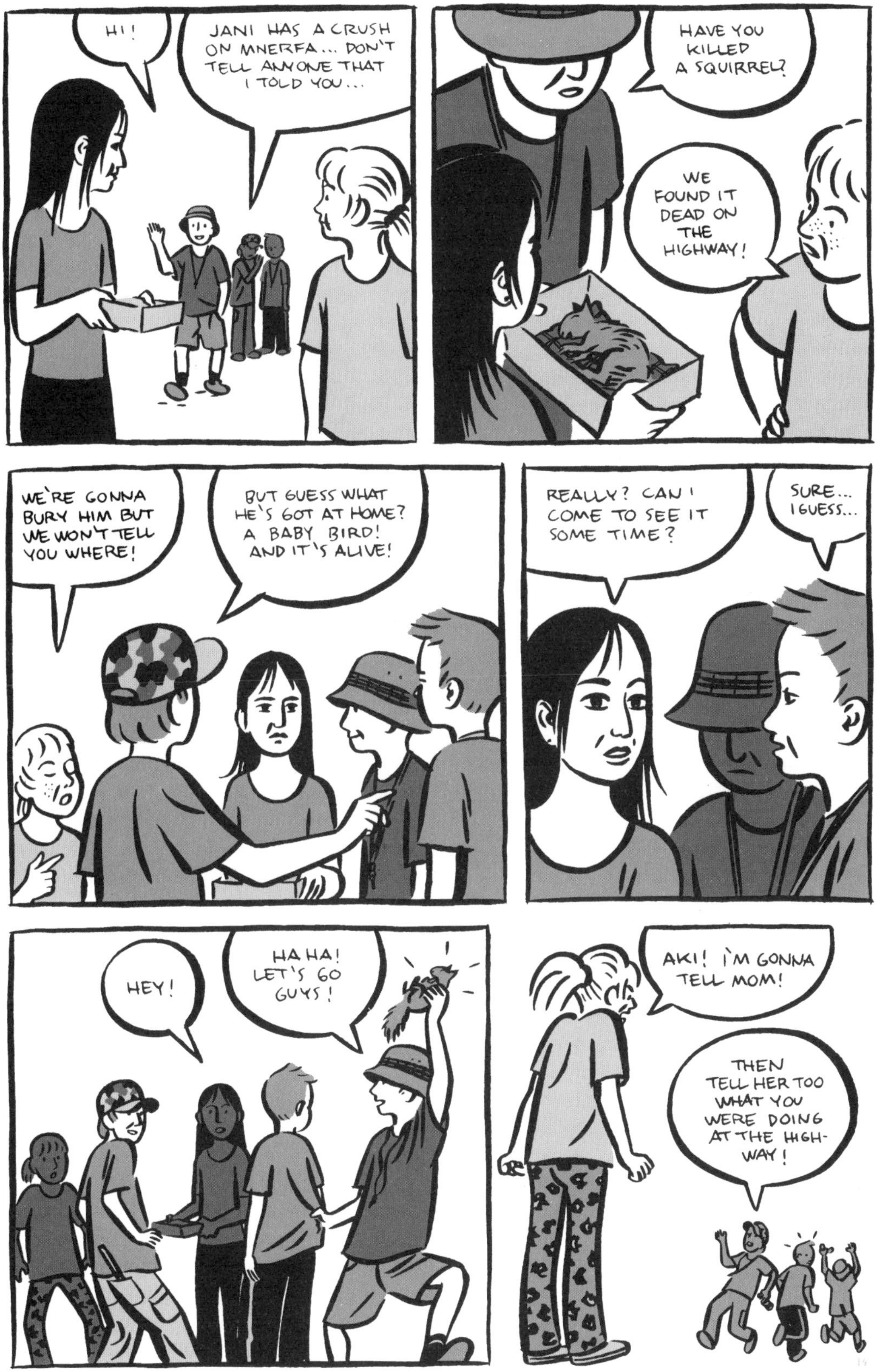
HI!
JANI HAS A CRUSH ON MNERFA... DON'T TELL ANYONE THAT I TOLD YOU...
HAVE YOU KILLED A SQUIRREL?
WE FOUND IT DEAD ON THE HIGHWAY!
WE'RE GONNA BURY HIM BUT WE WON'T TELL YOU WHERE!
BUT GUESS WHAT HE'S GOT AT HOME? A BABY BIRD! AND IT'S ALIVE!
REALLY? CAN I COME TO SEE IT SOME TIME?
SURE... I GUESS...
HEY!
HA HA! LET'S GO GUYS!
AKI! I'M GONNA TELL MOM!
THEN TELL HER TOO WHAT YOU WERE DOING AT THE HIGH-WAY!

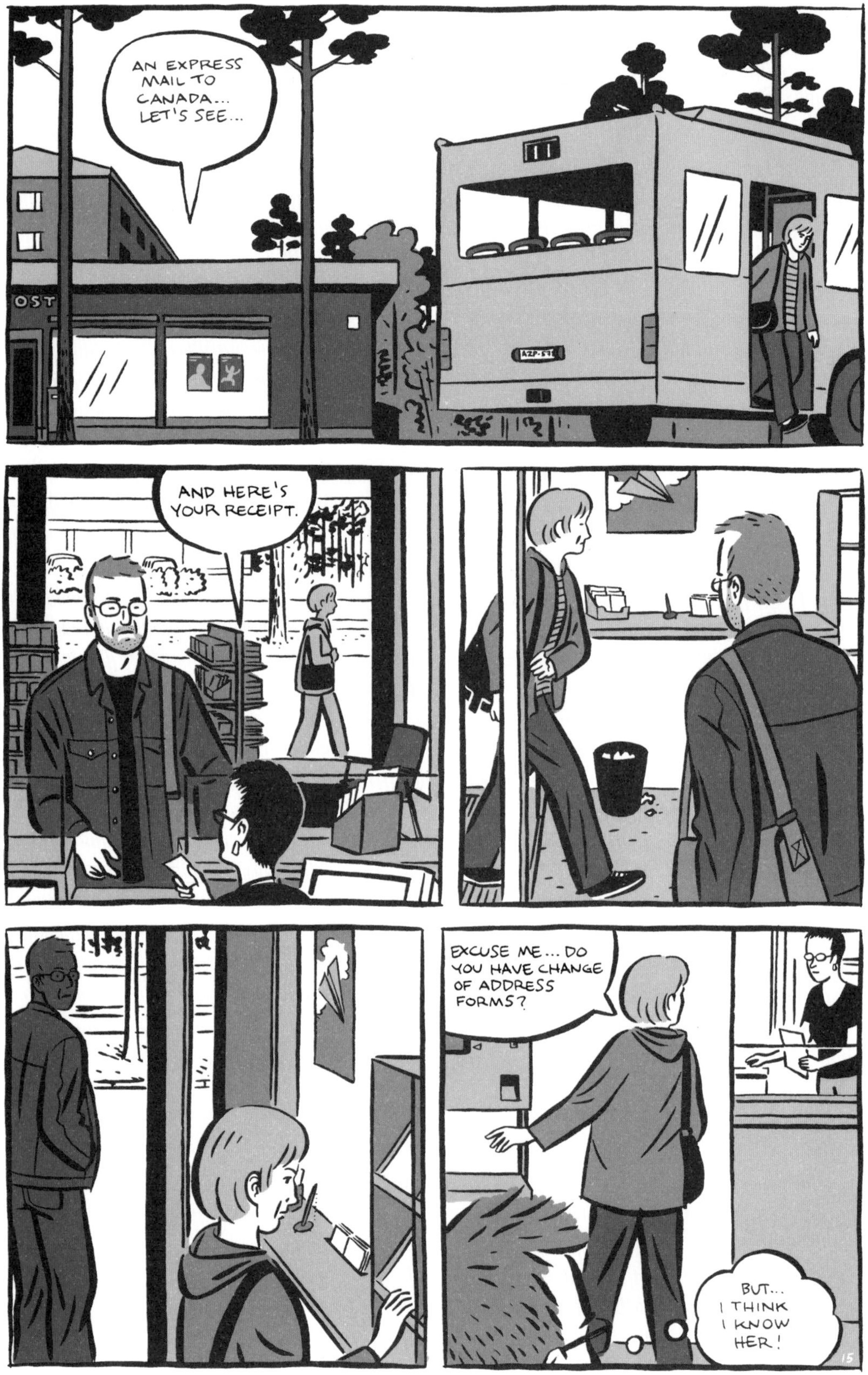
AN EXPRESS MAIL TO CANADA... LET'S SEE...
OST
AZP-573
AND HERE'S YOUR RECEIPT.
EXCUSE ME... DO YOU HAVE CHANGE OF ADDRESS FORMS?
BUT... I THINK I KNOW HER!
15

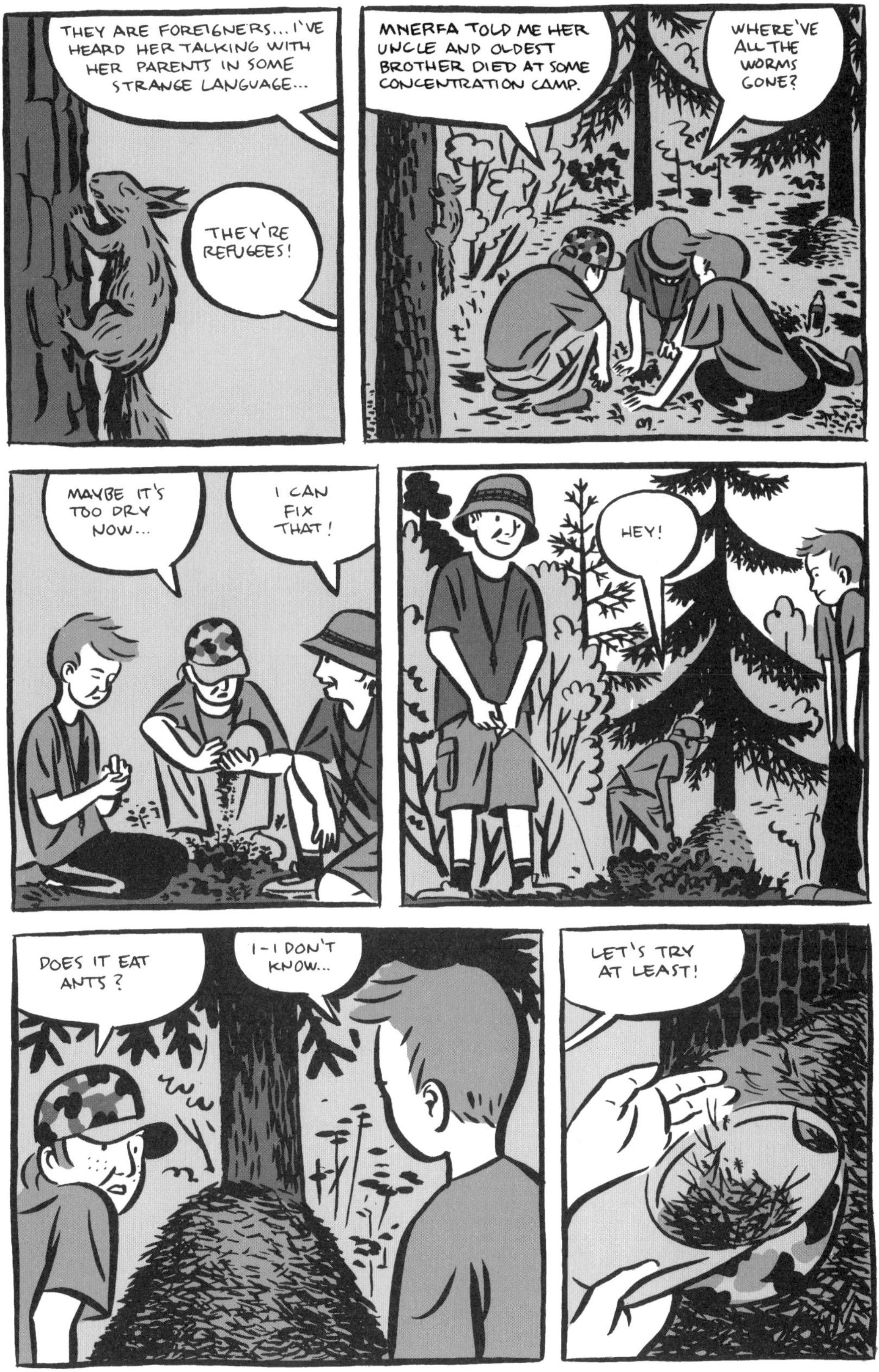
THEY ARE FOREIGNERS... I'VE HEARD HER TALKING WITH HER PARENTS IN SOME STRANGE LANGUAGE...
THEY'RE REFUGEES!
MNERFA TOLD ME HER UNCLE AND OLDEST BROTHER DIED AT SOME CONCENTRATION CAMP.
WHERE'VE ALL THE WORMS GONE?
MAYBE IT'S TOO DRY NOW...
I CAN FIX THAT!
HEY!
DOES IT EAT ANTS?
I-I DON'T KNOW...
LET'S TRY AT LEAST!

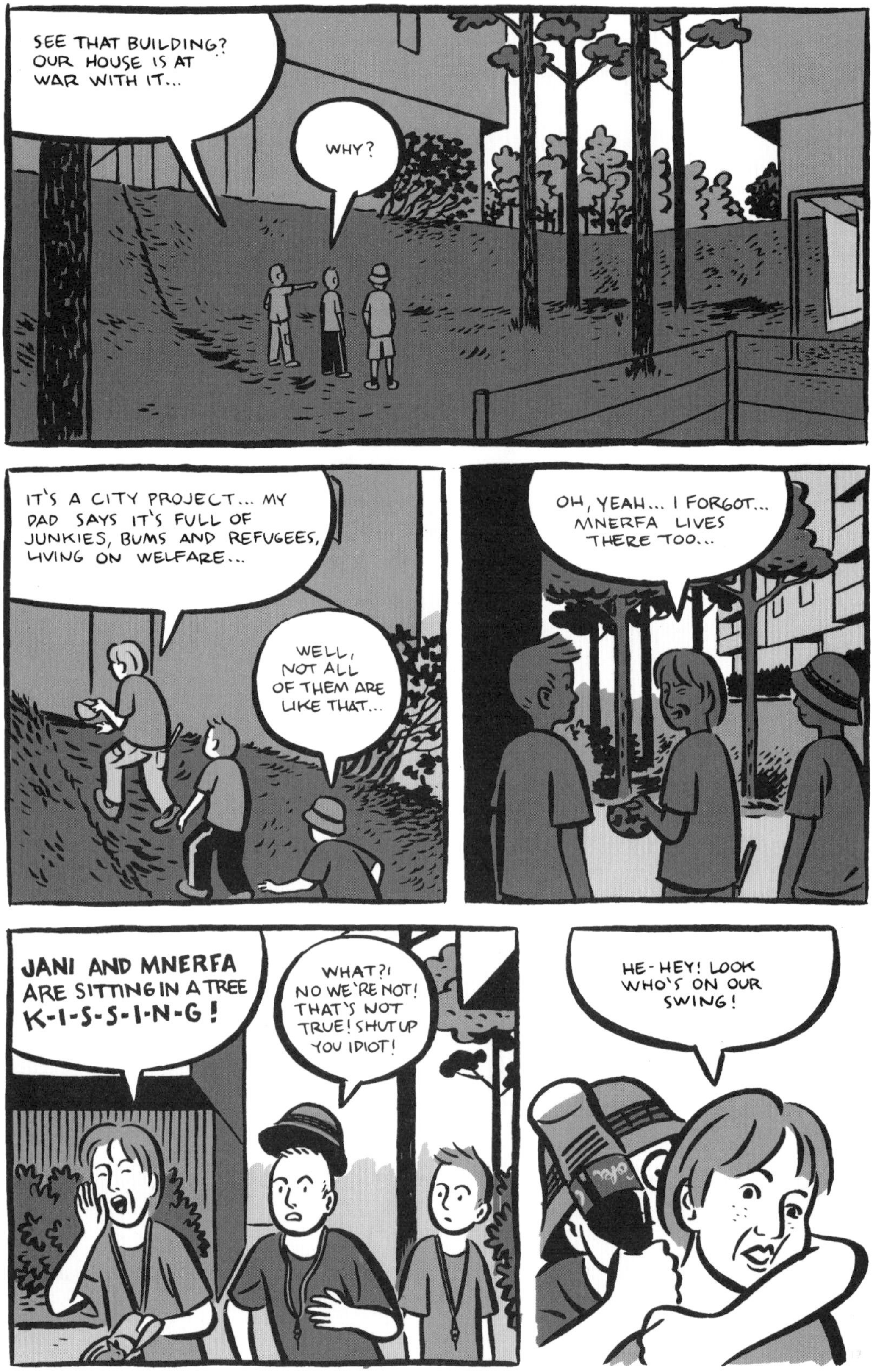
SEE THAT BUILDING? OUR HOUSE IS AT WAR WITH IT...
WHY?
IT'S A CITY PROJECT... MY DAD SAYS IT'S FULL OF JUNKIES, BUMS AND REFUGEES, LIVING ON WELFARE...
WELL, NOT ALL OF THEM ARE LIKE THAT...
OH, YEAH... I FORGOT... MNERFA LIVES THERE TOO...
JANI AND MNERFA ARE SITTING IN A TREE K-I-S-S-I-N-G!
WHAT?! NO WE'RE NOT! THAT'S NOT TRUE! SHUT UP YOU IDIOT!
HE-HEY! LOOK WHO'S ON OUR SWING!

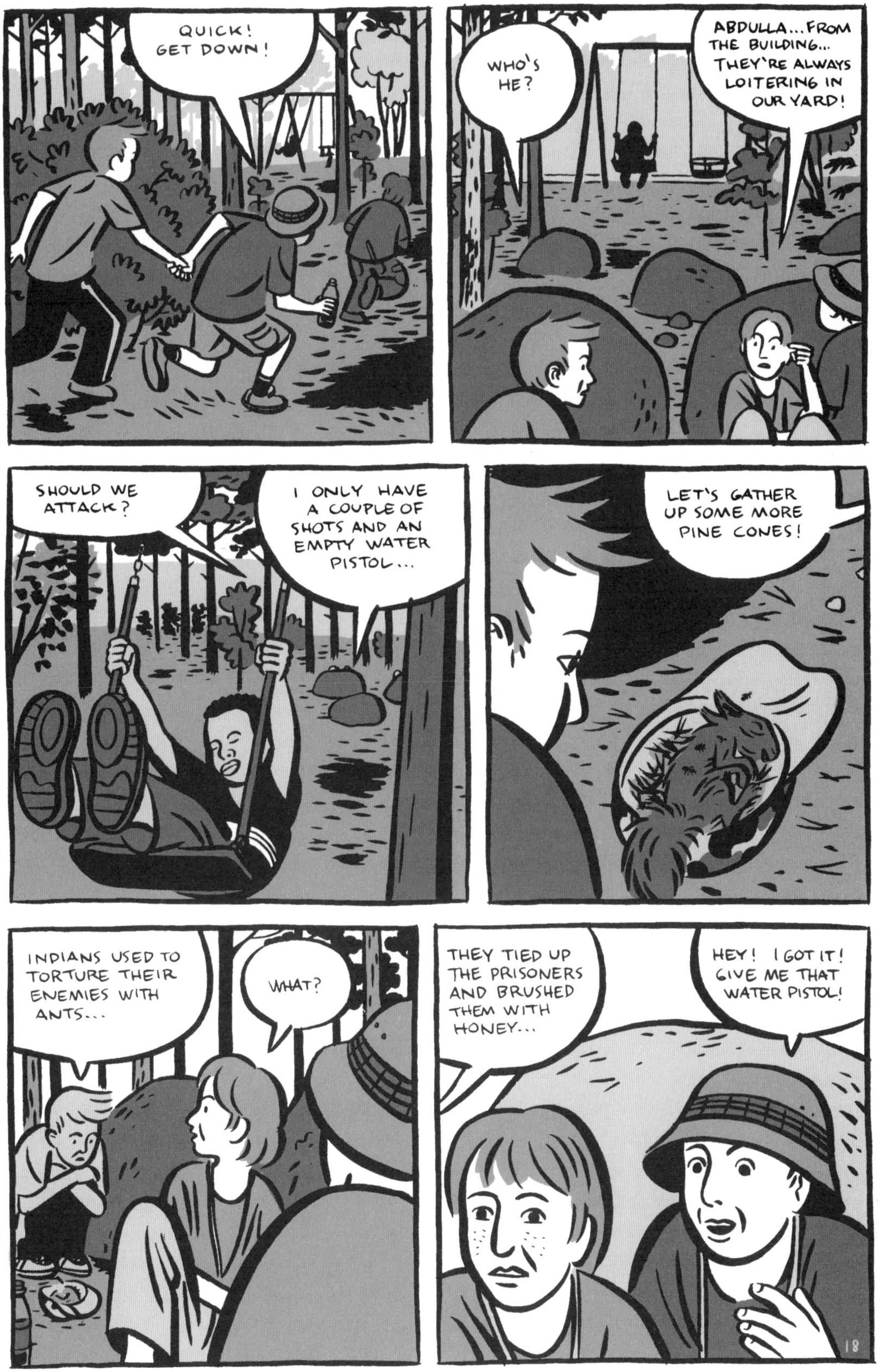
QUICK! GET DOWN!
WHO'S HE?
ABDULLA... FROM THE BUILDING... THEY'RE ALWAYS LOITERING IN OUR YARD!
SHOULD WE ATTACK?
I ONLY HAVE A COUPLE OF SHOTS AND AN EMPTY WATER PISTOL...
LET'S GATHER UP SOME MORE PINE CONES!
INDIANS USED TO TORTURE THEIR ENEMIES WITH ANTS...
WHAT?
THEY TIED UP THE PRISONERS AND BRUSHED THEM WITH HONEY...
HEY! I GOT IT! GIVE ME THAT WATER PISTOL!
18

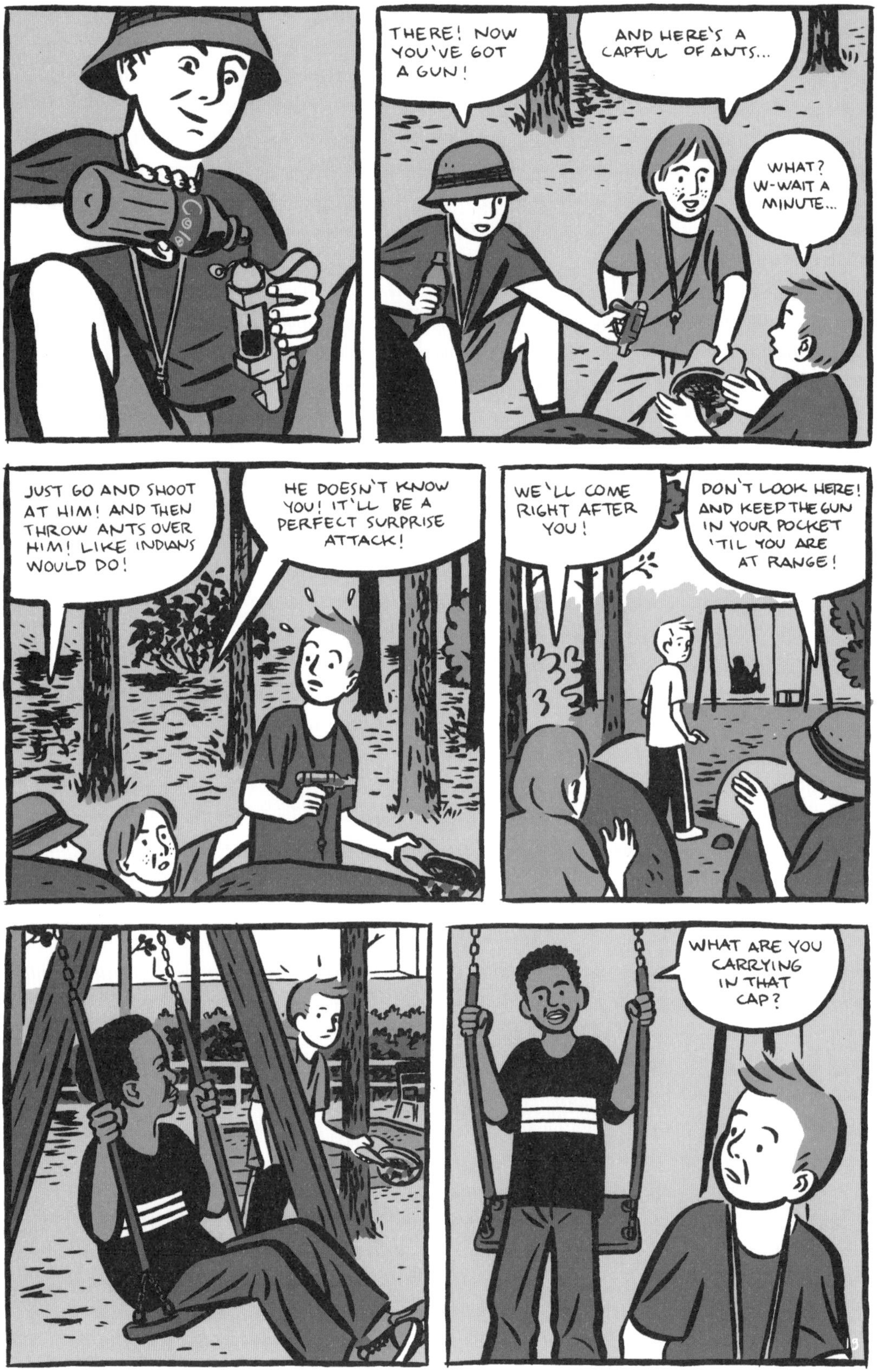
THERE! NOW YOU'VE GOT A GUN!
AND HERE'S A CAPFUL OF ANTS...
WHAT? W-WAIT A MINUTE...
JUST GO AND SHOOT AT HIM! AND THEN THROW ANTS OVER HIM! LIKE INDIANS WOULD DO!
HE DOESN'T KNOW YOU! IT'LL BE A PERFECT SURPRISE ATTACK!
WE'LL COME RIGHT AFTER YOU!
DON'T LOOK HERE! AND KEEP THE GUN IN YOUR POCKET 'TIL YOU ARE AT RANGE!
WHAT ARE YOU CARRYING IN THAT CAP?
19

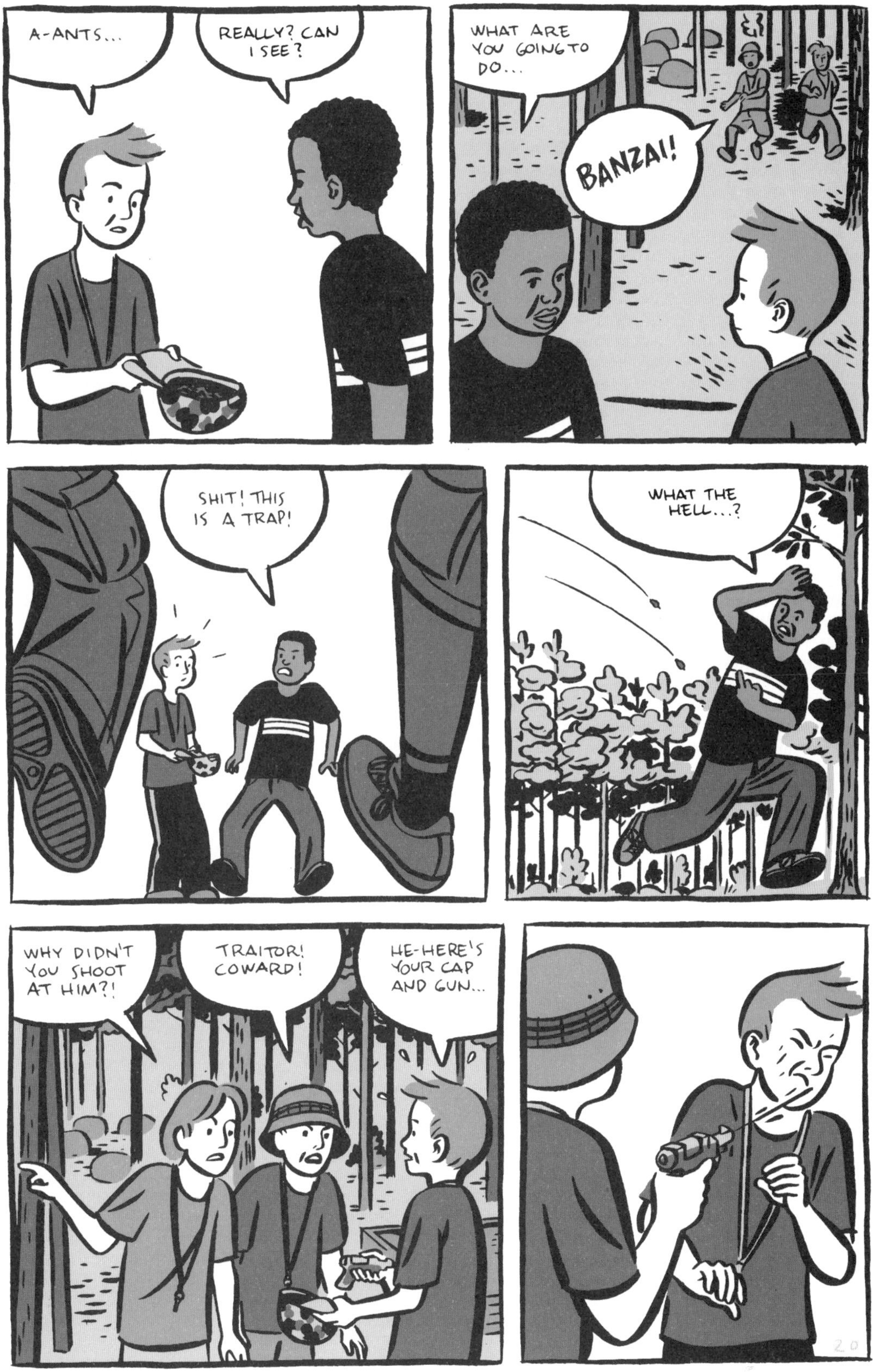
A-ANTS...
REALLY? CAN I SEE?
WHAT ARE YOU GOING TO DO...
BANZAI!
SHIT! THIS IS A TRAP!
WHAT THE HELL...?
WHY DIDN'T YOU SHOOT AT HIM?!
TRAITOR! COWARD!
HE-HERE'S YOUR CAP AND GUN...
20

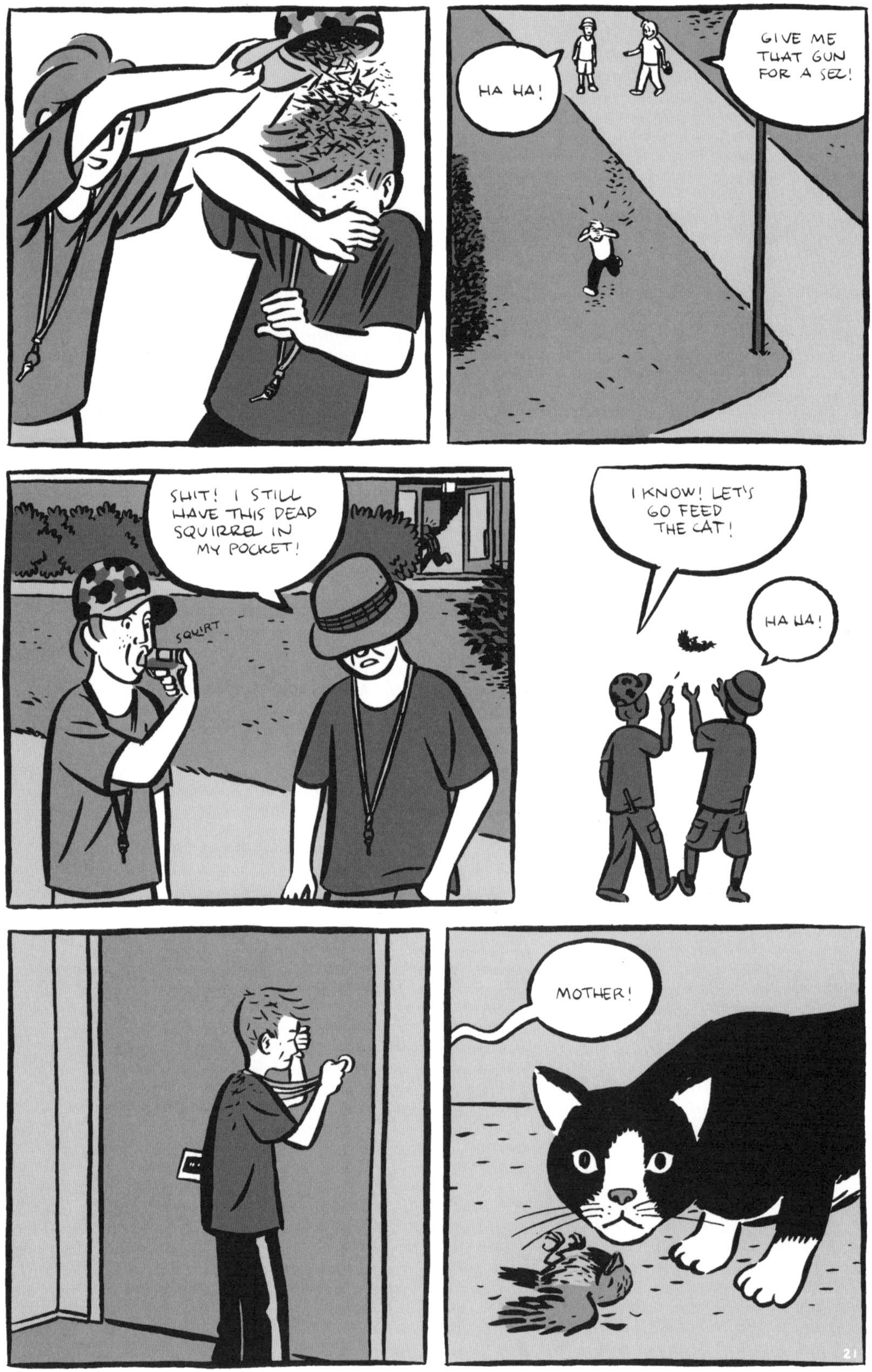
HA HA!
GIVE ME THAT GUN FOR A SEC!
SHIT! I STILL HAVE THIS DEAD SQUIRREL IN MY POCKET!
SQUIRT
I KNOW! LET'S GO FEED THE CAT!
HA HA!
MOTHER!

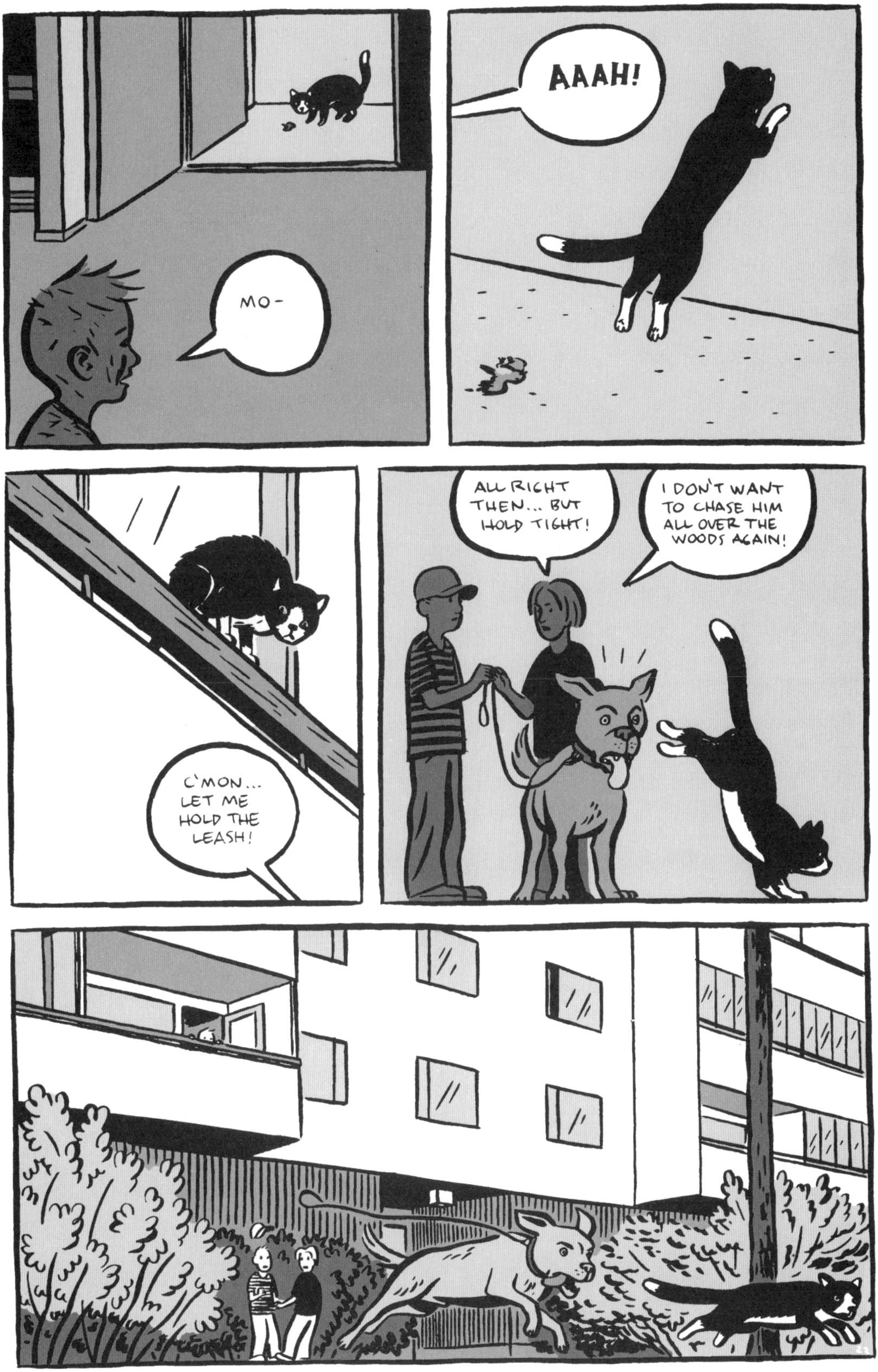
MO-
AAAH!
C'MON... LET ME HOLD THE LEASH!
ALL RIGHT THEN... BUT HOLD TIGHT!
I DON'T WANT TO CHASE HIM ALL OVER THE WOODS AGAIN!

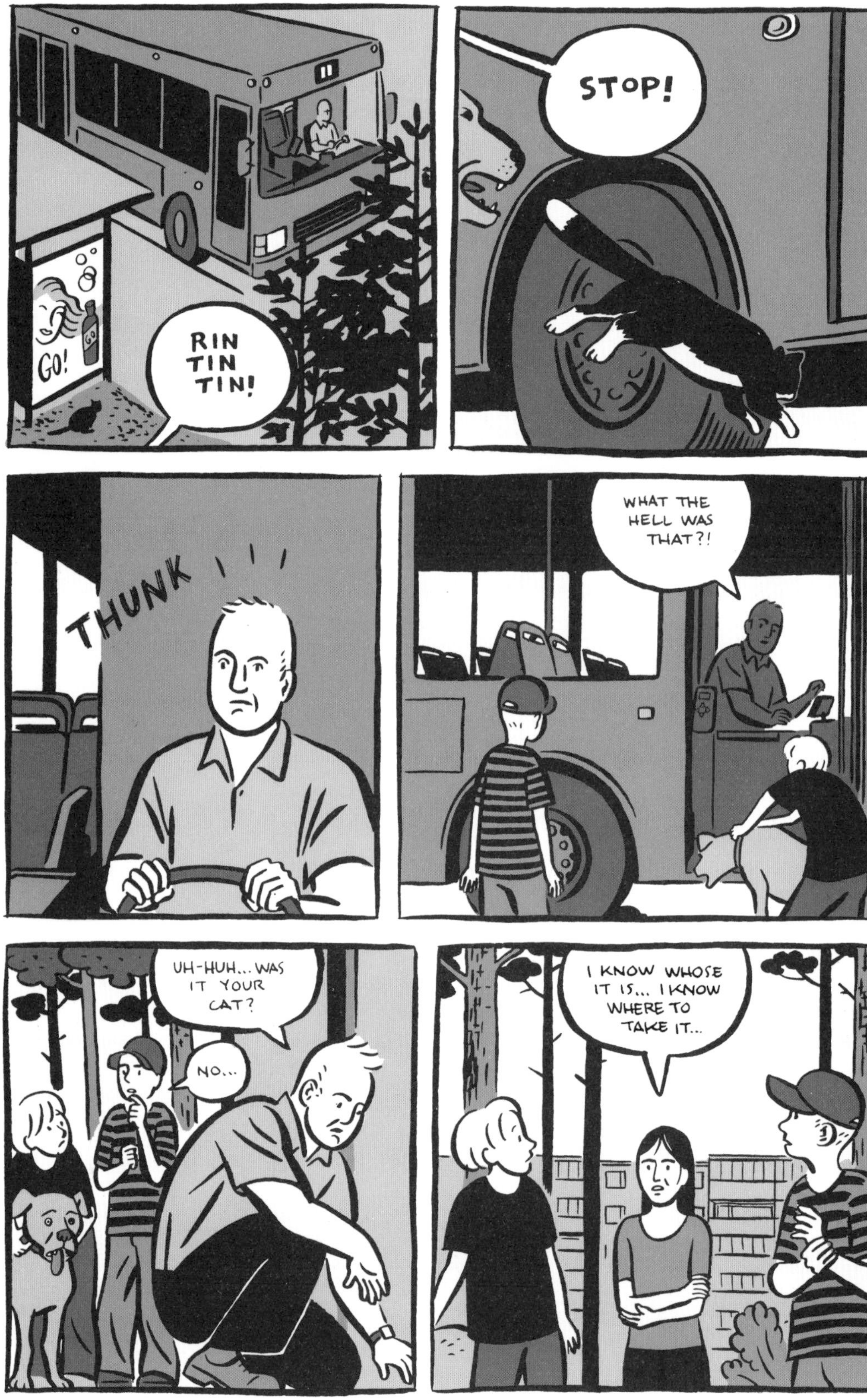
GO!
RIN TIN TIN!
STOP!
THUNK
WHAT THE HELL WAS THAT?!
UH-HUH... WAS IT YOUR CAT?
NO...
I KNOW WHOSE IT IS... I KNOW WHERE TO TAKE IT...

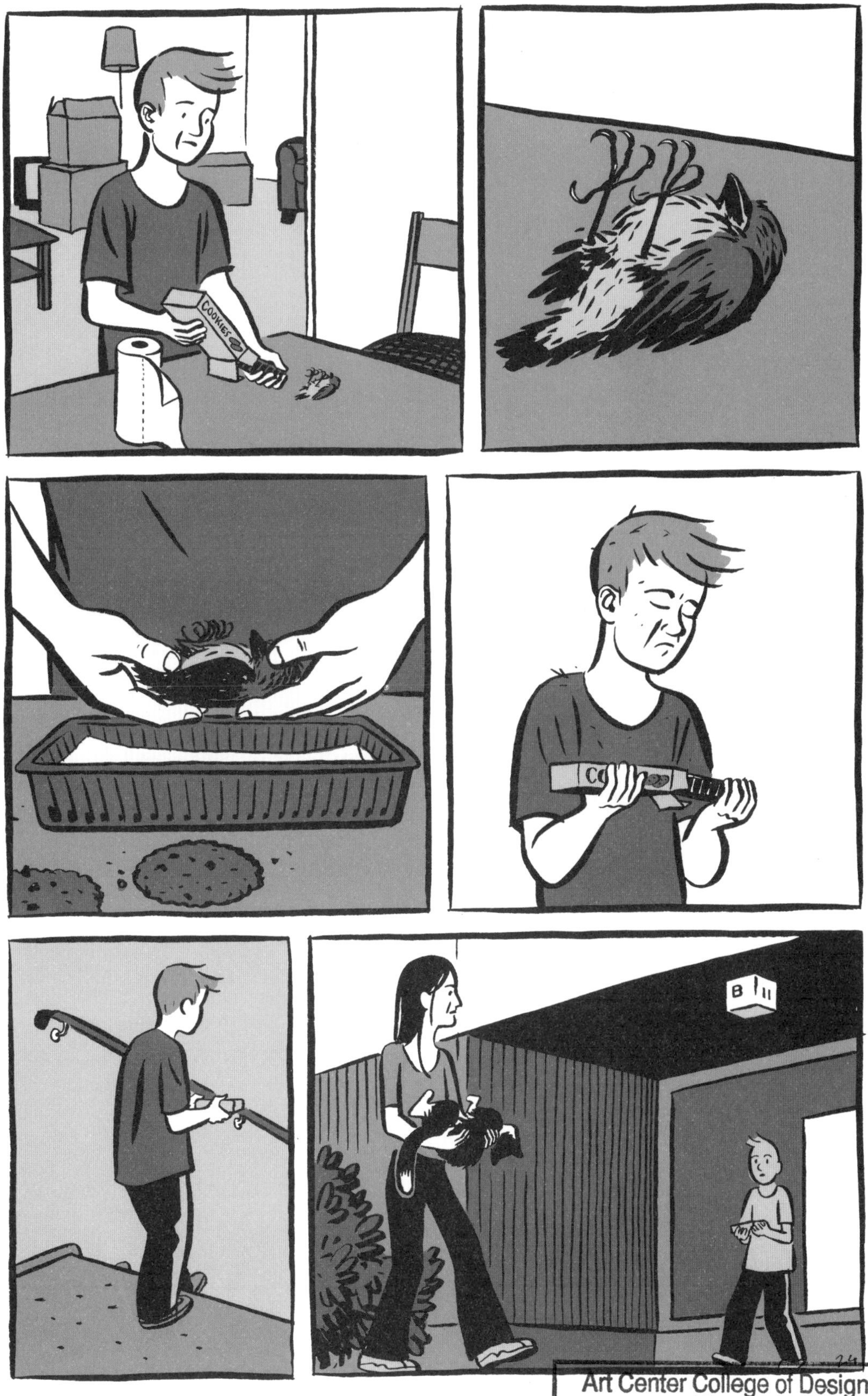
COOKIES

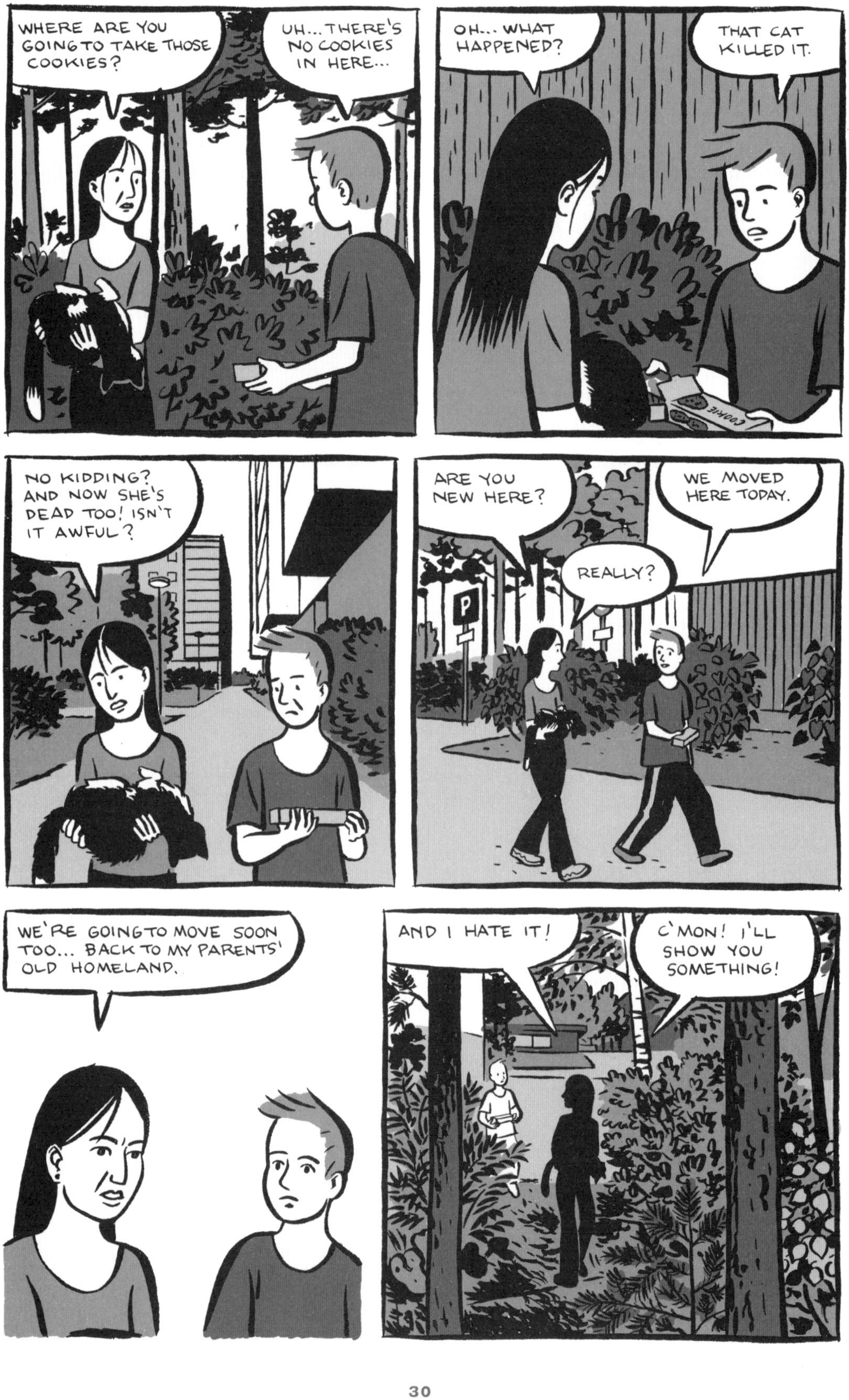
WHERE ARE YOU GOING TO TAKE THOSE COOKIES?
UH... THERE'S NO COOKIES IN HERE...
OH... WHAT HAPPENED?
THAT CAT KILLED IT.
COOKIE
NO KIDDING? AND NOW SHE'S DEAD TOO! ISN'T IT AWFUL?
ARE YOU NEW HERE?
WE MOVED HERE TODAY.
REALLY?
P
WE'RE GOING TO MOVE SOON TOO... BACK TO MY PARENTS' OLD HOMELAND.
AND I HATE IT!
C'MON! I'LL SHOW YOU SOMETHING!

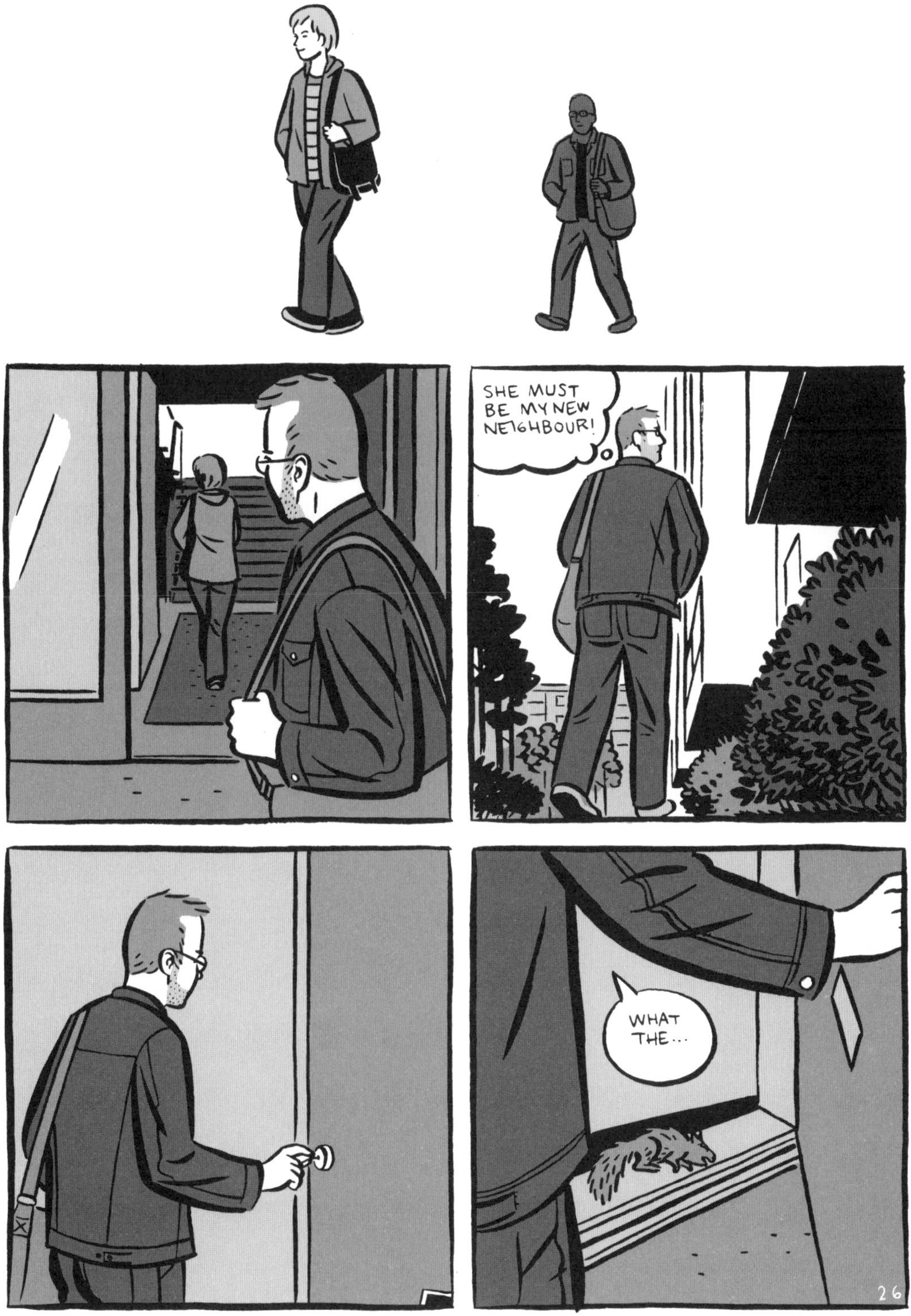
SHE MUST BE MY NEW NEIGHBOUR!
WHAT THE...
26

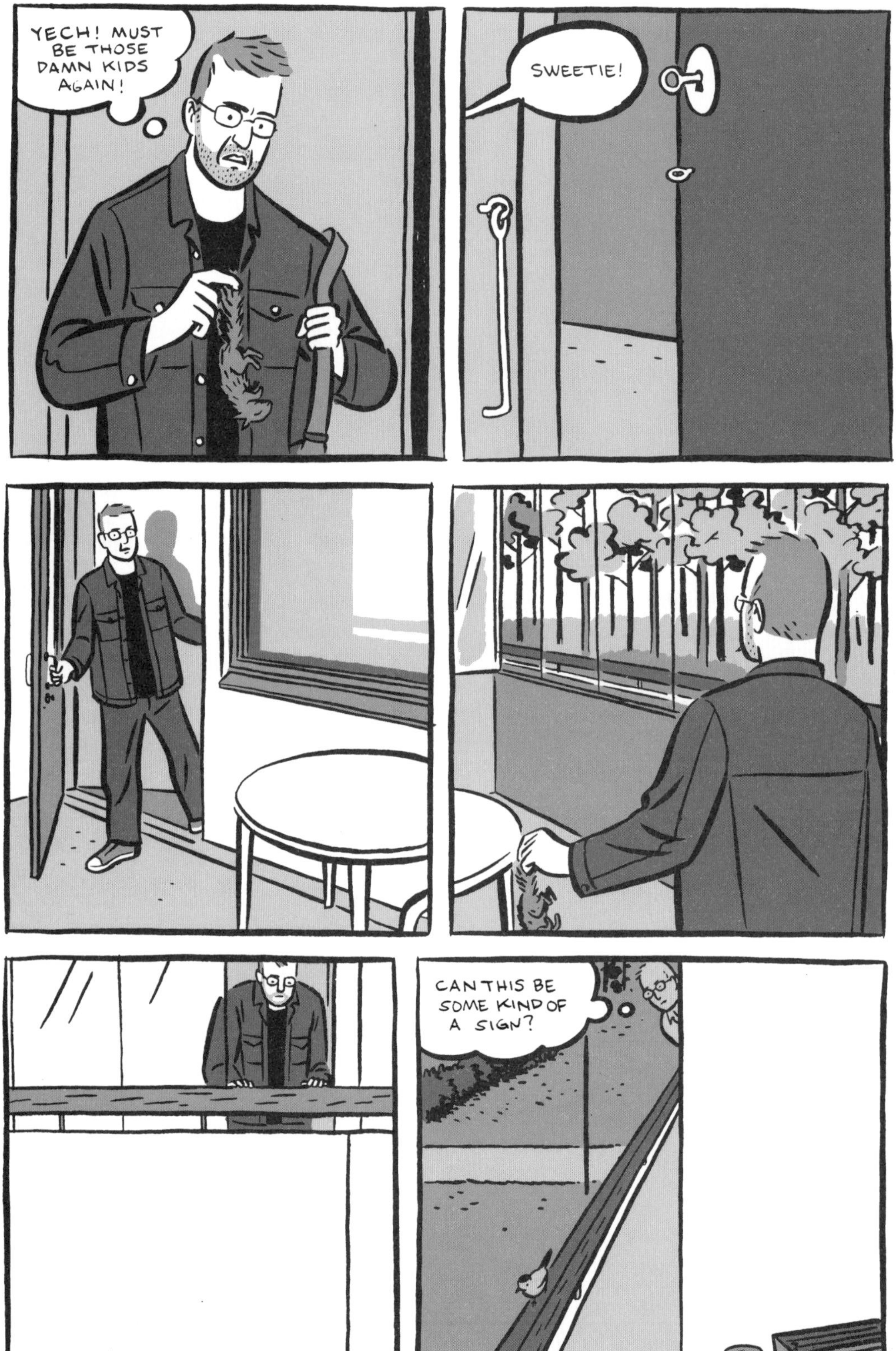

YECH! MUST BE THOSE DAMN KIDS AGAIN!
SWEETIE!
CAN THIS BE SOME KIND OF A SIGN?

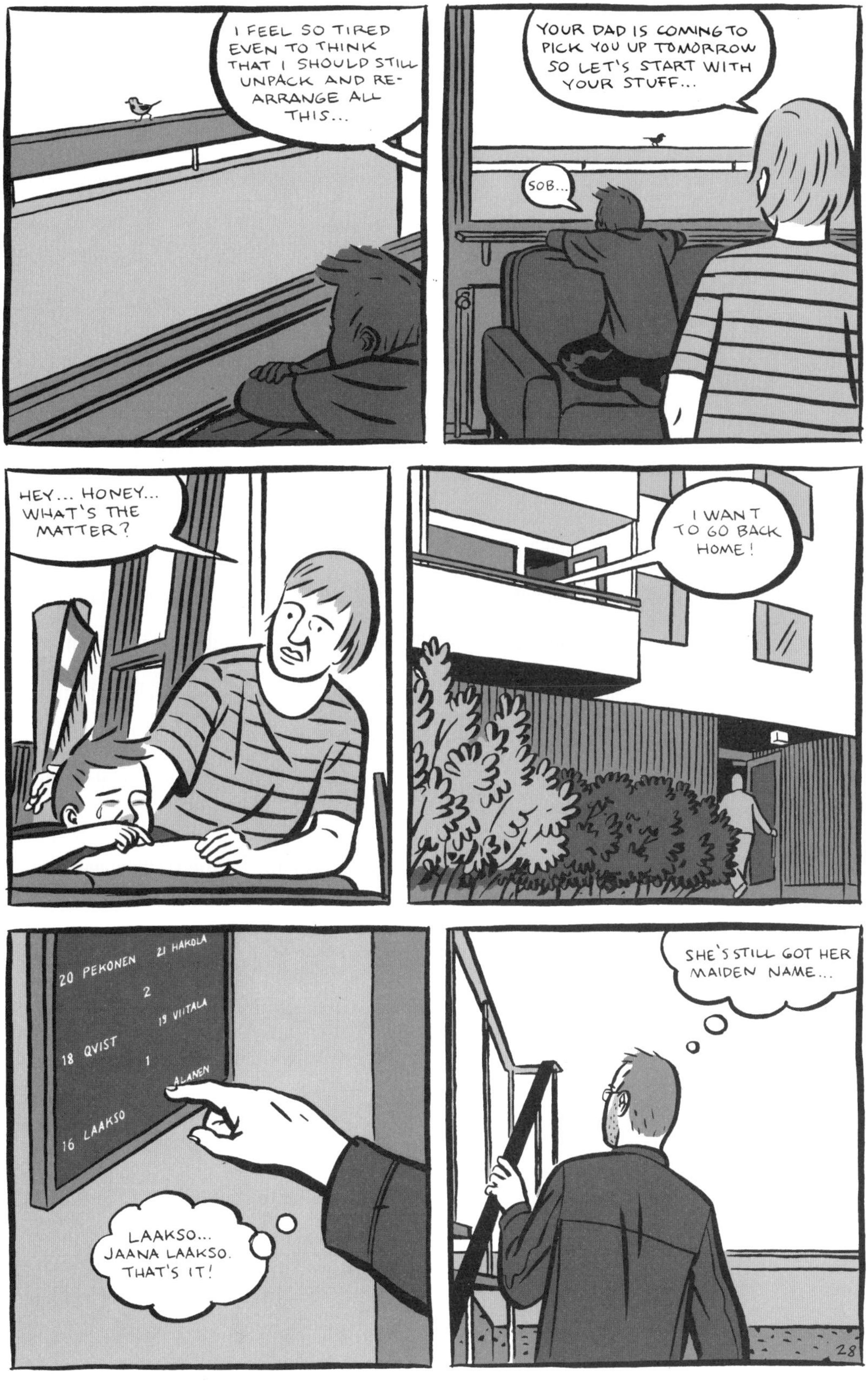
I FEEL SO TIRED EVEN TO THINK THAT I SHOULD STILL UNPACK AND RE-ARRANGE ALL THIS...
YOUR DAD IS COMING TO PICK YOU UP TOMORROW SO LET'S START WITH YOUR STUFF...
SOB...
HEY... HONEY... WHAT'S THE MATTER?
I WANT TO GO BACK HOME!
20 PEKONEN
21 HAKOLA
2
19 VIITALA
18 QVIST
1
ALANEN
16 LAAKSO
LAAKSO... JAANA LAAKSO. THAT'S IT!
SHE'S STILL GOT HER MAIDEN NAME...
28

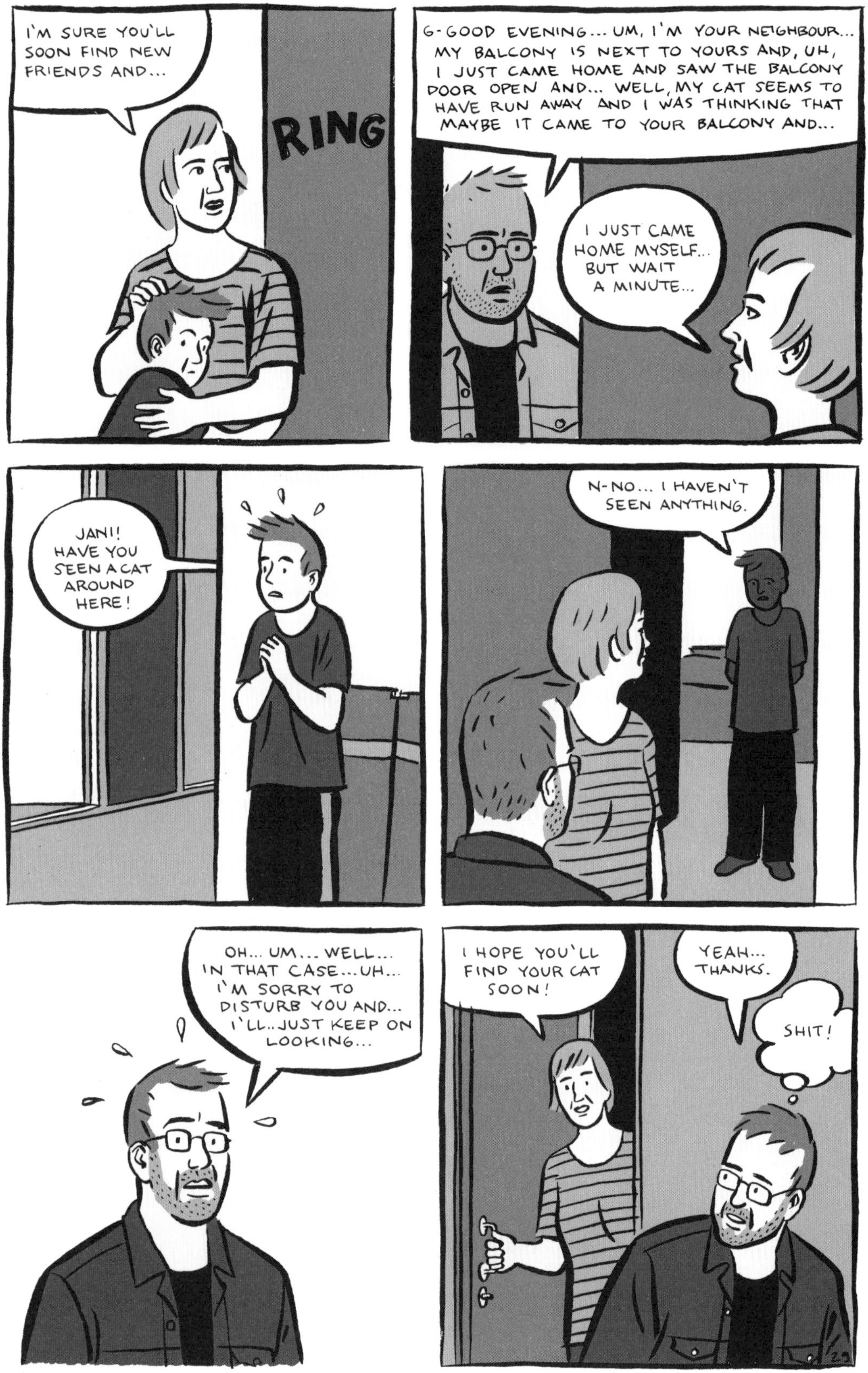
I'M SURE YOU'LL SOON FIND NEW FRIENDS AND...
RING
G-GOOD EVENING... UM, I'M YOUR NEIGHBOUR... MY BALCONY IS NEXT TO YOURS AND, UH, I JUST CAME HOME AND SAW THE BALCONY DOOR OPEN AND... WELL, MY CAT SEEMS TO HAVE RUN AWAY AND I WAS THINKING THAT MAYBE IT CAME TO YOUR BALCONY AND...
I JUST CAME HOME MYSELF... BUT WAIT A MINUTE...
JANI! HAVE YOU SEEN A CAT AROUND HERE!
N-NO... I HAVEN'T SEEN ANYTHING.
OH... UM... WELL... IN THAT CASE... UH... I'M SORRY TO DISTURB YOU AND... I'LL.. JUST KEEP ON LOOKING...
I HOPE YOU'LL FIND YOUR CAT SOON!
YEAH... THANKS.
SHIT!

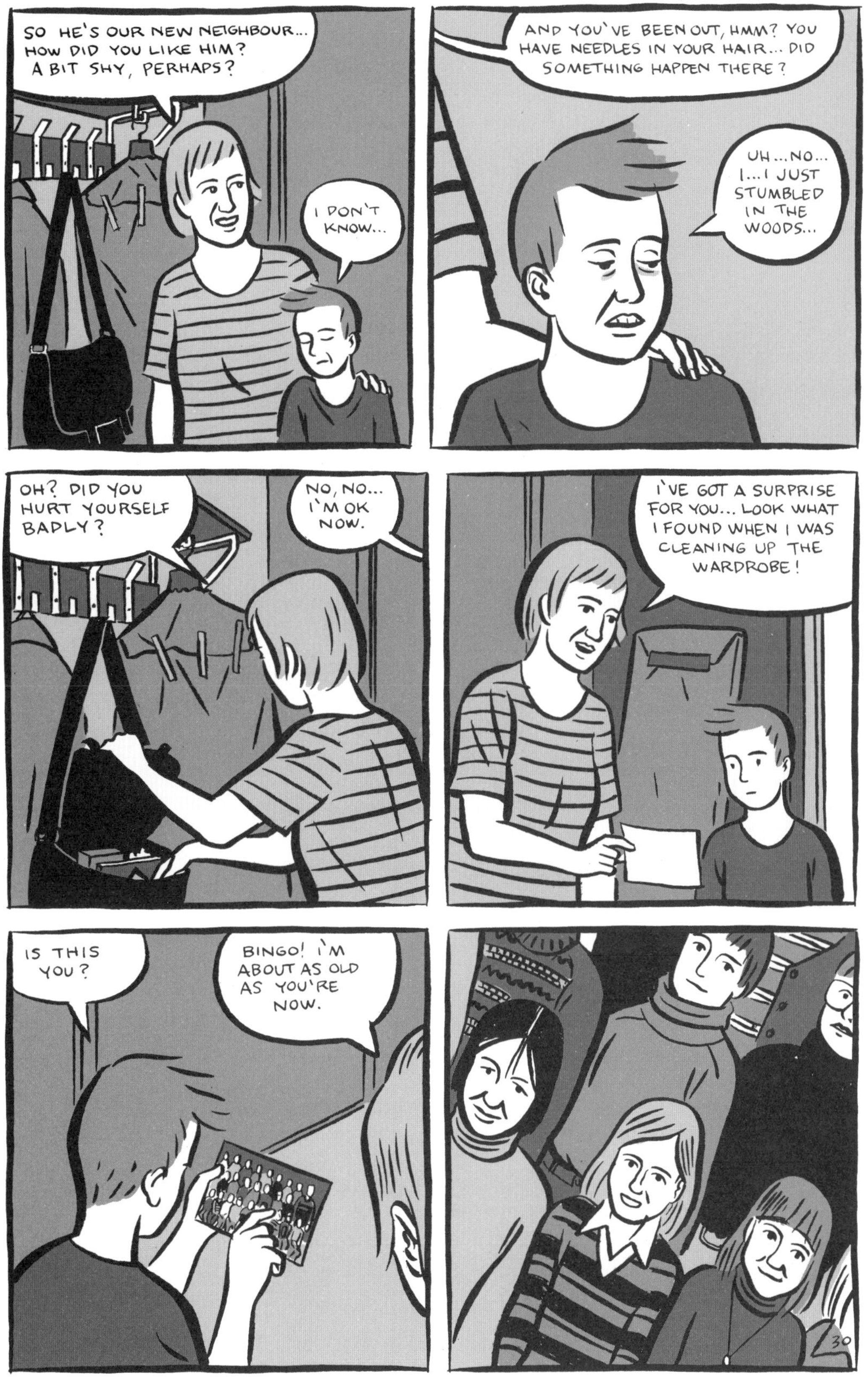
SO HE'S OUR NEW NEIGHBOUR... HOW DID YOU LIKE HIM? A BIT SHY, PERHAPS?
I DON'T KNOW...
AND YOU'VE BEEN OUT, HMM? YOU HAVE NEEDLES IN YOUR HAIR... DID SOMETHING HAPPEN THERE?
UH... NO... I... I JUST STUMBLED IN THE WOODS...
OH? DID YOU HURT YOURSELF BADLY?
NO, NO... I'M OK NOW.
I'VE GOT A SURPRISE FOR YOU... LOOK WHAT I FOUND WHEN I WAS CLEANING UP THE WARDROBE!
IS THIS YOU?
BINGO! I'M ABOUT AS OLD AS YOU'RE NOW.
30

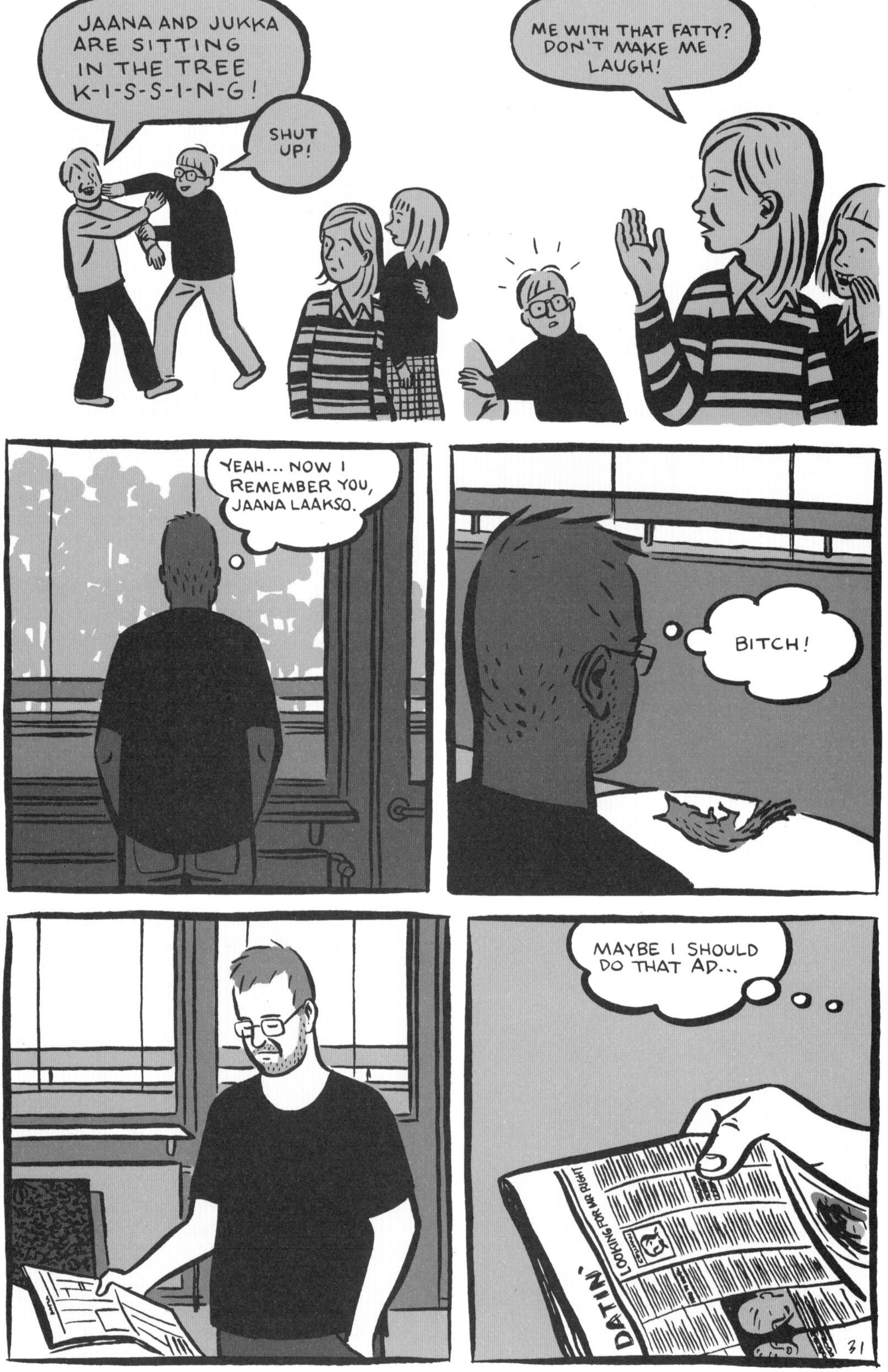
JAANA AND JUKKA ARE SITTING IN THE TREE K-I-S-S-I-N-G!
SHUT UP!
ME WITH THAT FATTY? DON'T MAKE ME LAUGH!
YEAH... NOW I REMEMBER YOU, JAANA LAAKSO.
BITCH!
MAYBE I SHOULD DO THAT AD...
DATIN'
LOOKING FOR MR RIGHT
31

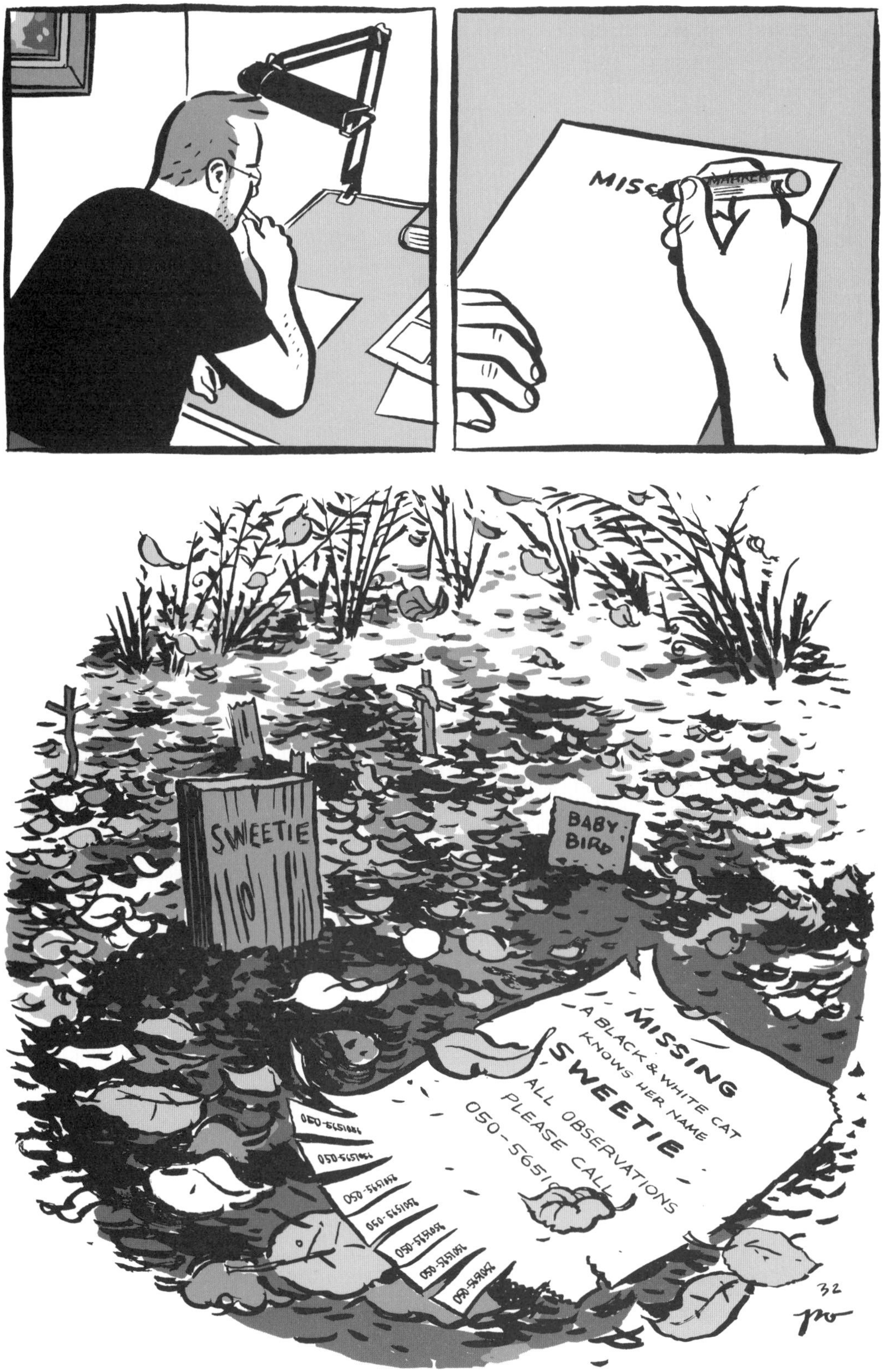
MISS
MARKER
SWEETIE
BABY BIRD
MISSING
A BLACK & WHITE CAT
KNOWS HER NAME
SWEETIE
ALL OBSERVATIONS
PLEASE CALL
050-5651
32

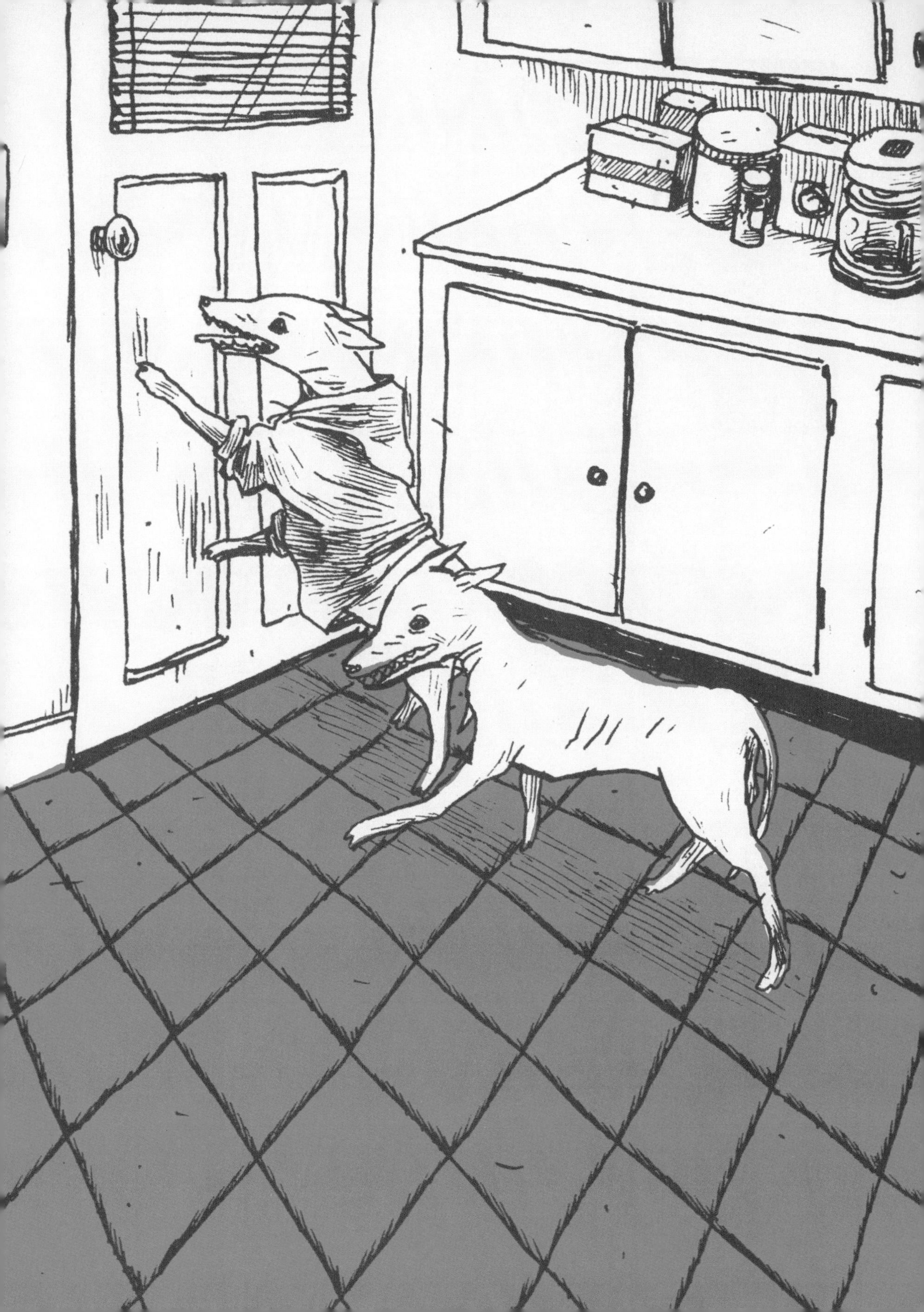

Jeffrey Brown

Jeffrey Brown was born in Grand Rapids, Michigan in 1975. After years of drawing, he moved to Chicago in 2000 to pursue an MFA at the School Of The Art Institute. While there he gave up painting to begin drawing comics, inspired by fellow Chicago cartoonist Chris Ware. His first work was CLUMSY, an autobiographical novel about a long distance relationship which has been widely acclaimed, and was featured in a segment on the NPR radio show THIS AMERICAN LIFE.

Since then Jeffrey has continued to produce comics at a steady pace, following with the story of losing his virginity in his second book UNLIKELY as well as numerous mini-comics and anthology contributions. His current projects include a superhero parody and plans for a more ambitious autobiographical novel detailing his adolescence.

Based on actual events

MONDAY NIGHTMARE

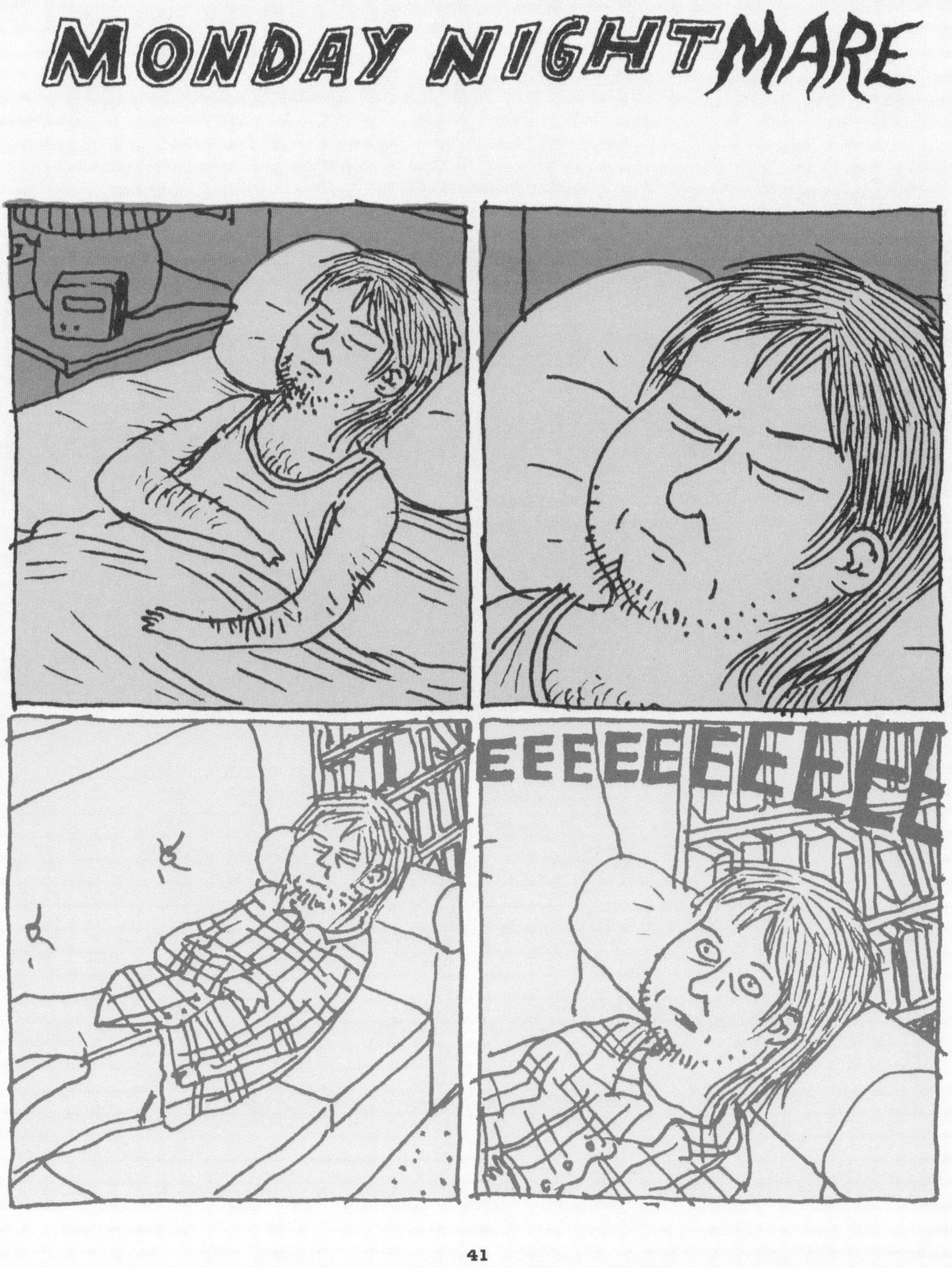
EEEEEEEE

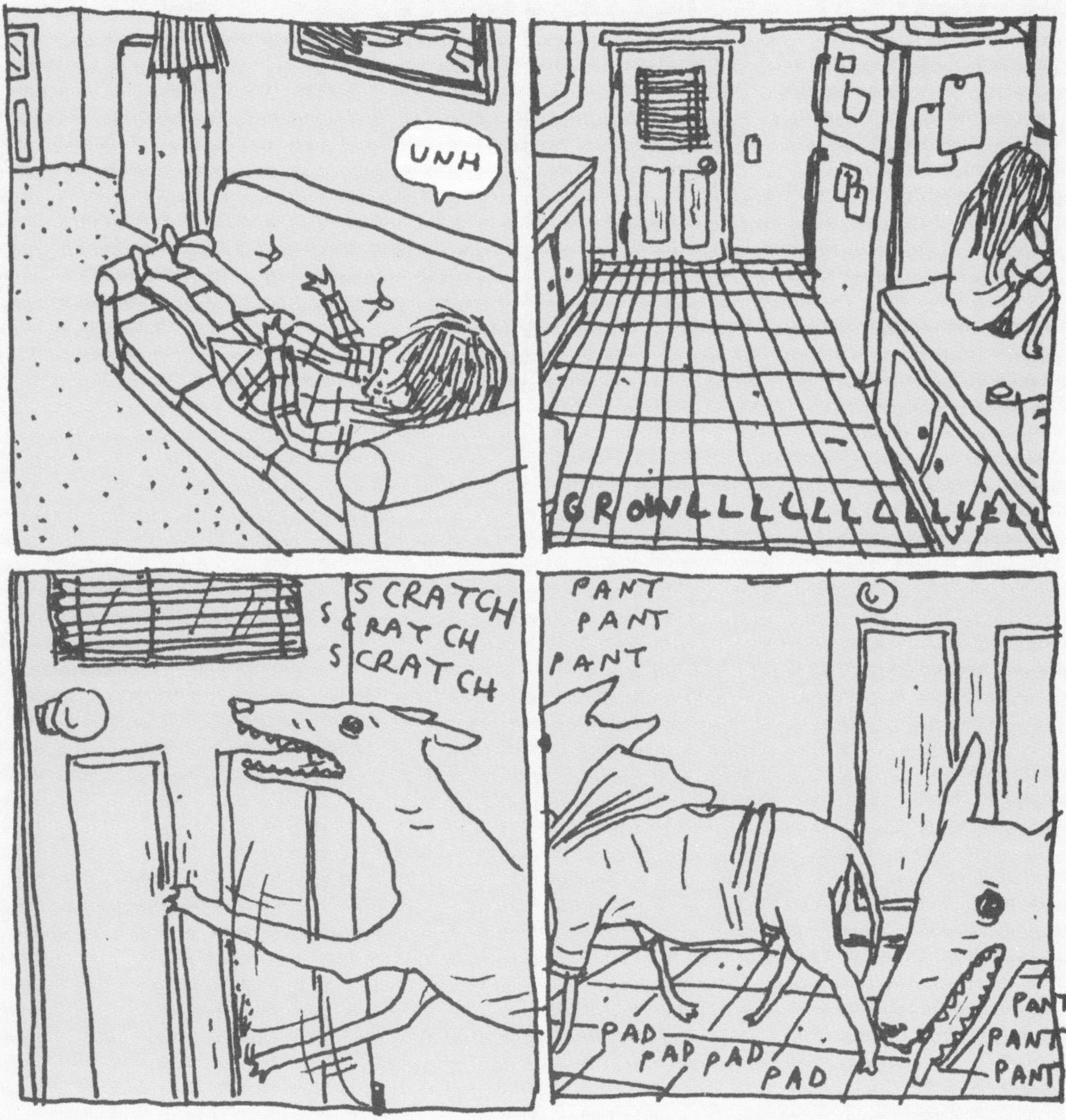
UNH
GROWLLLLLLLLLLLLL
SCRATCH
SCRATCH
SCRATCH
PANT
PANT
PANT
PAD
PAD PAD
PAD
PANT
PANT
PANT

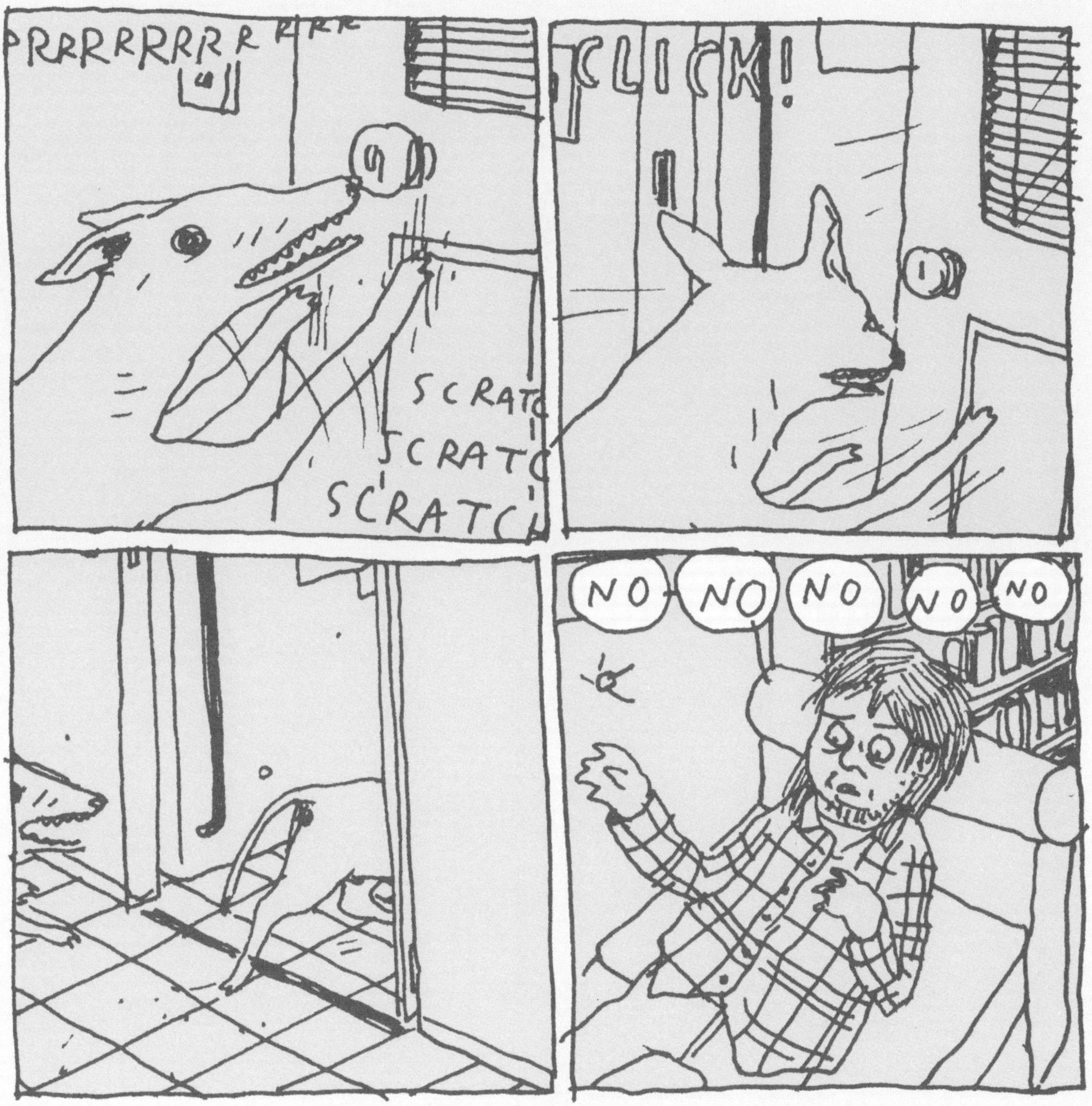
PRRRRRRRRRRR
SCRATC
SCRATC
SCRATCH
CLICK!
NO
NO
NO
NO
NO

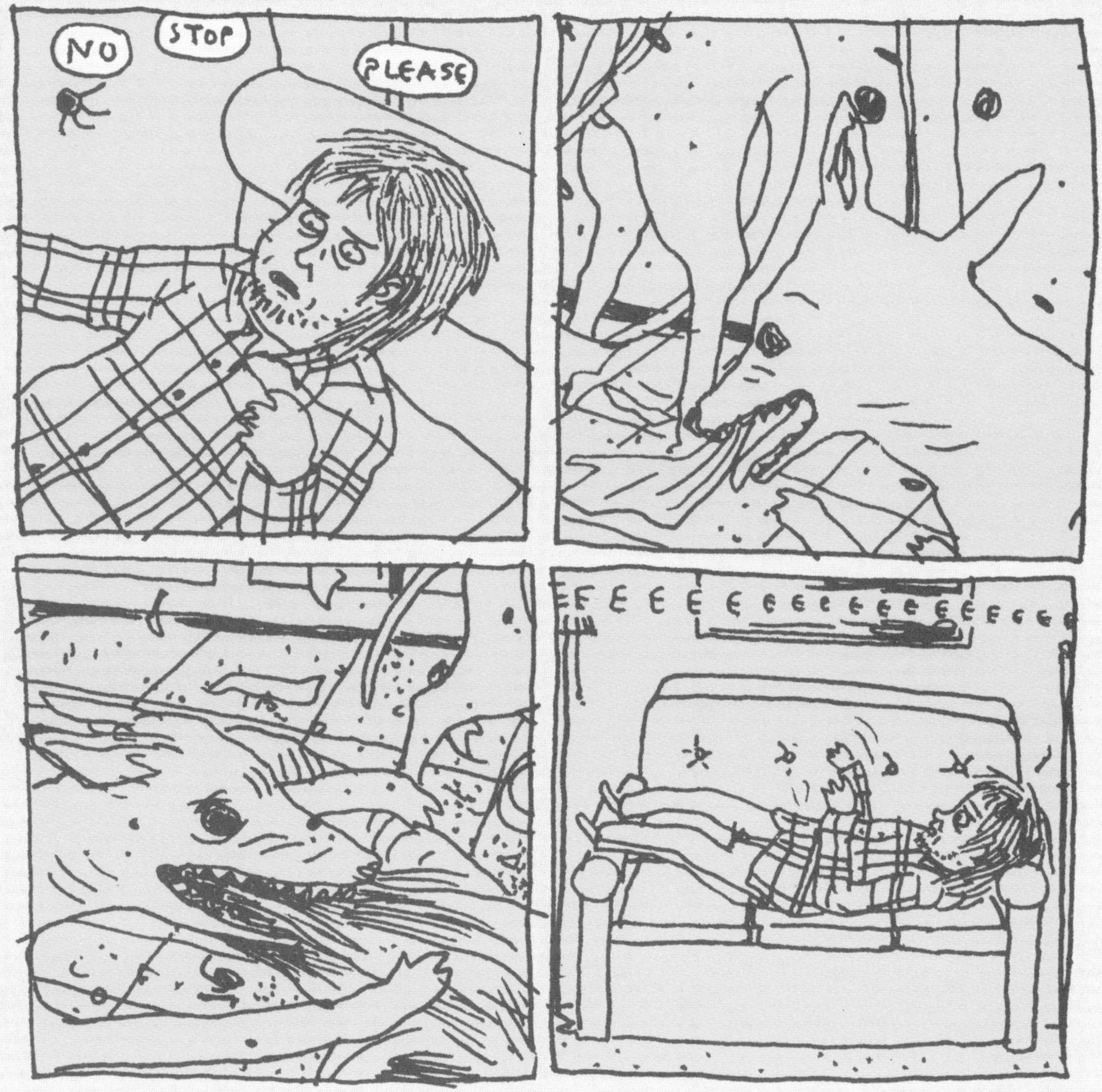
NO
STOP
PLEASE
EEEEEEEEEEEEEEEEEE

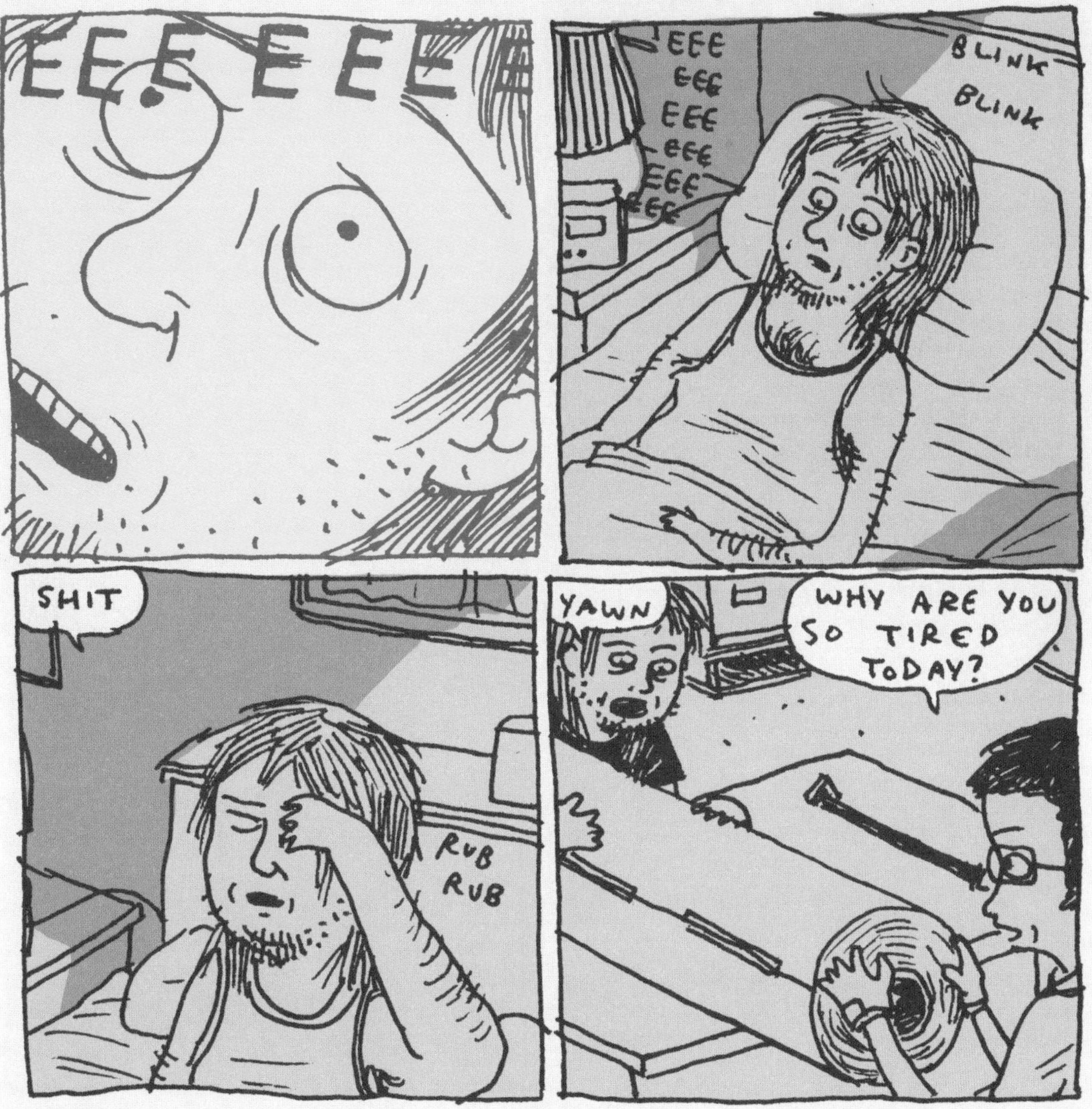
EEE EEE
EEE
EEE
EEE
EEE
EEE
EEE
BLINK
BLINK
SHIT
RUB
RUB
YAWN
WHY ARE YOU SO TIRED TODAY?

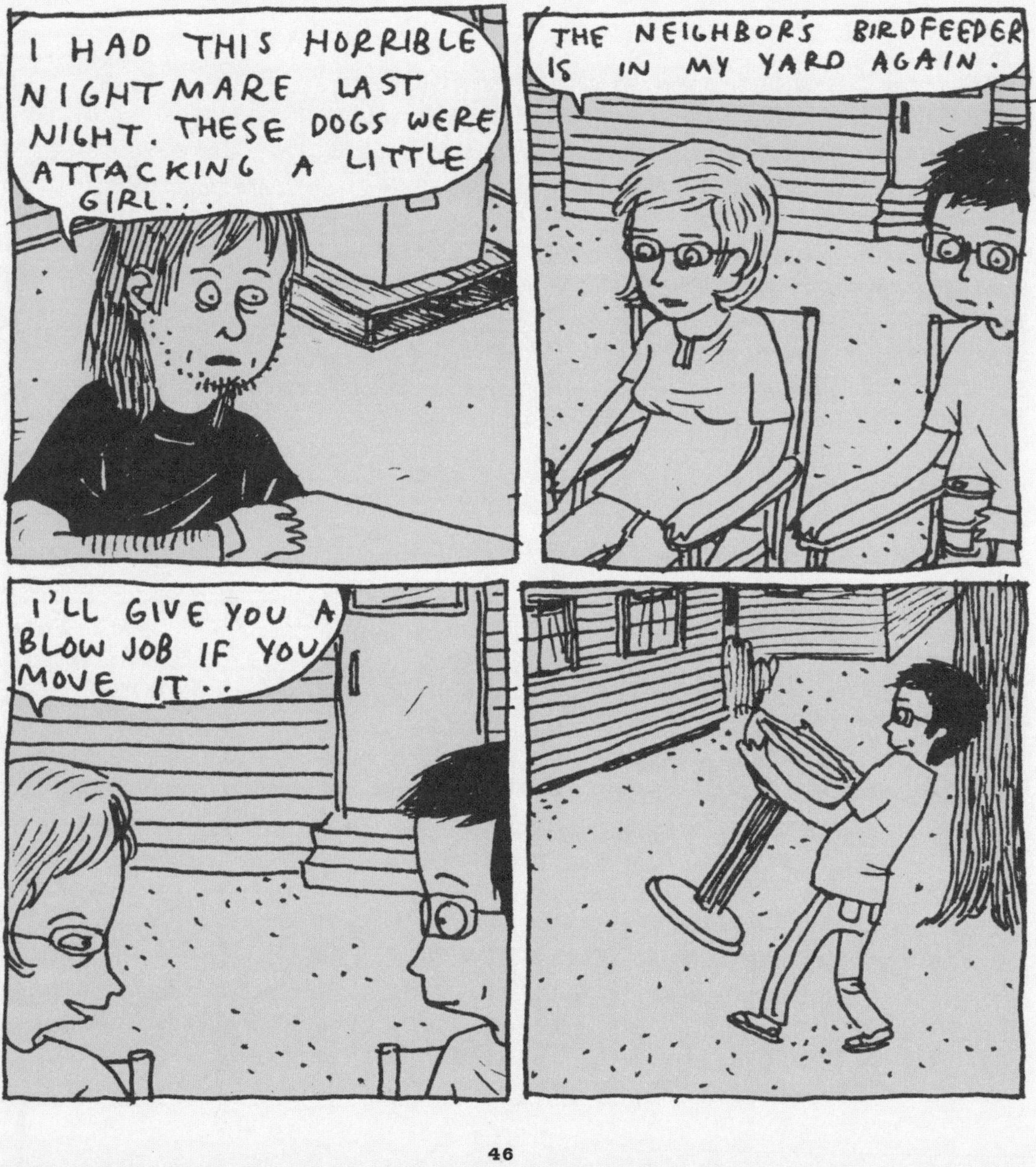
I HAD THIS HORRIBLE NIGHTMARE LAST NIGHT. THESE DOGS WERE ATTACKING A LITTLE GIRL...
THE NEIGHBOR'S BIRDFEEDER IS IN MY YARD AGAIN.
I'LL GIVE YOU A BLOW JOB IF YOU MOVE IT..

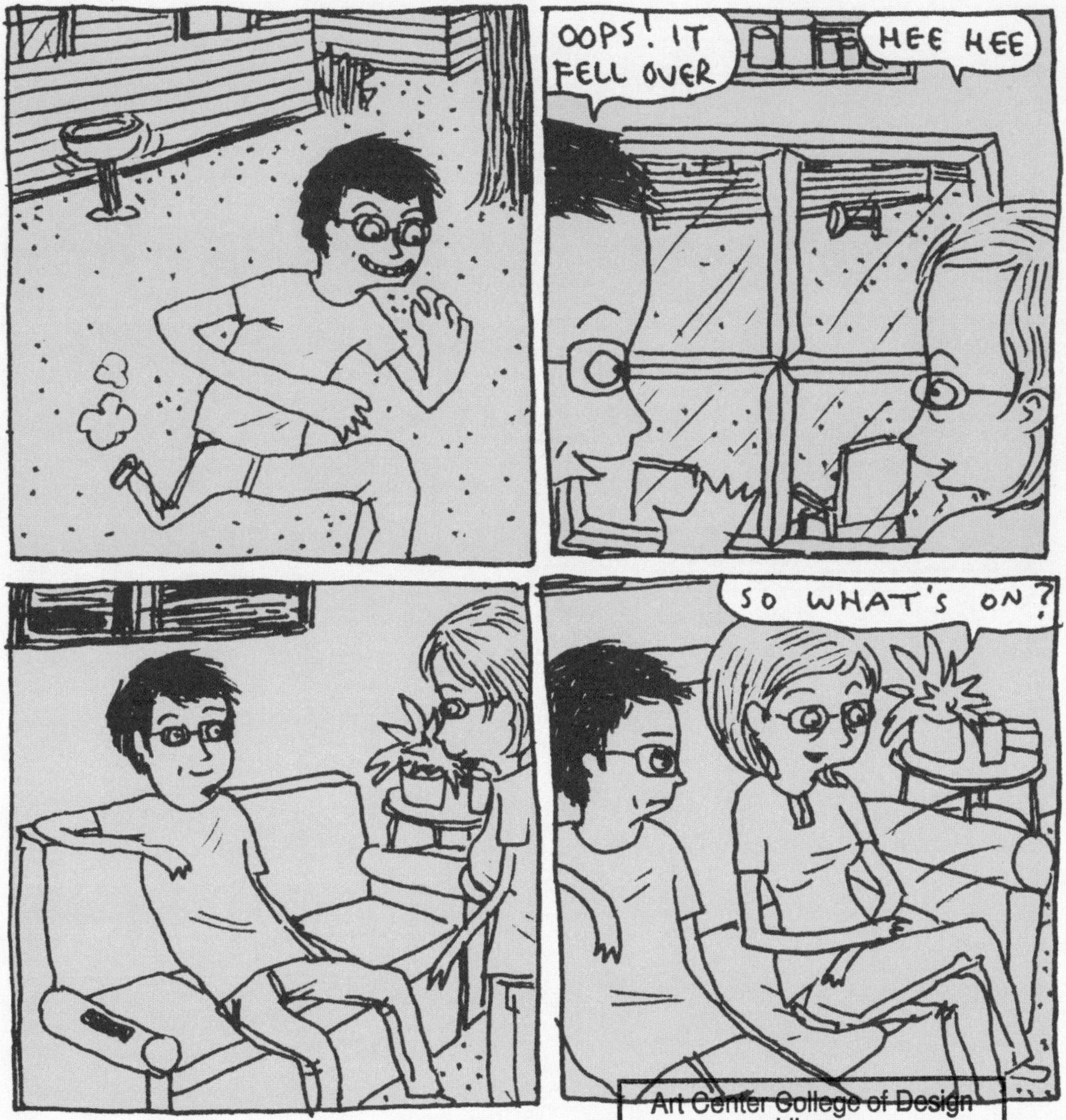
OOPS! IT FELL OVER
HEE HEE
SO WHAT'S ON?

TUESDAY

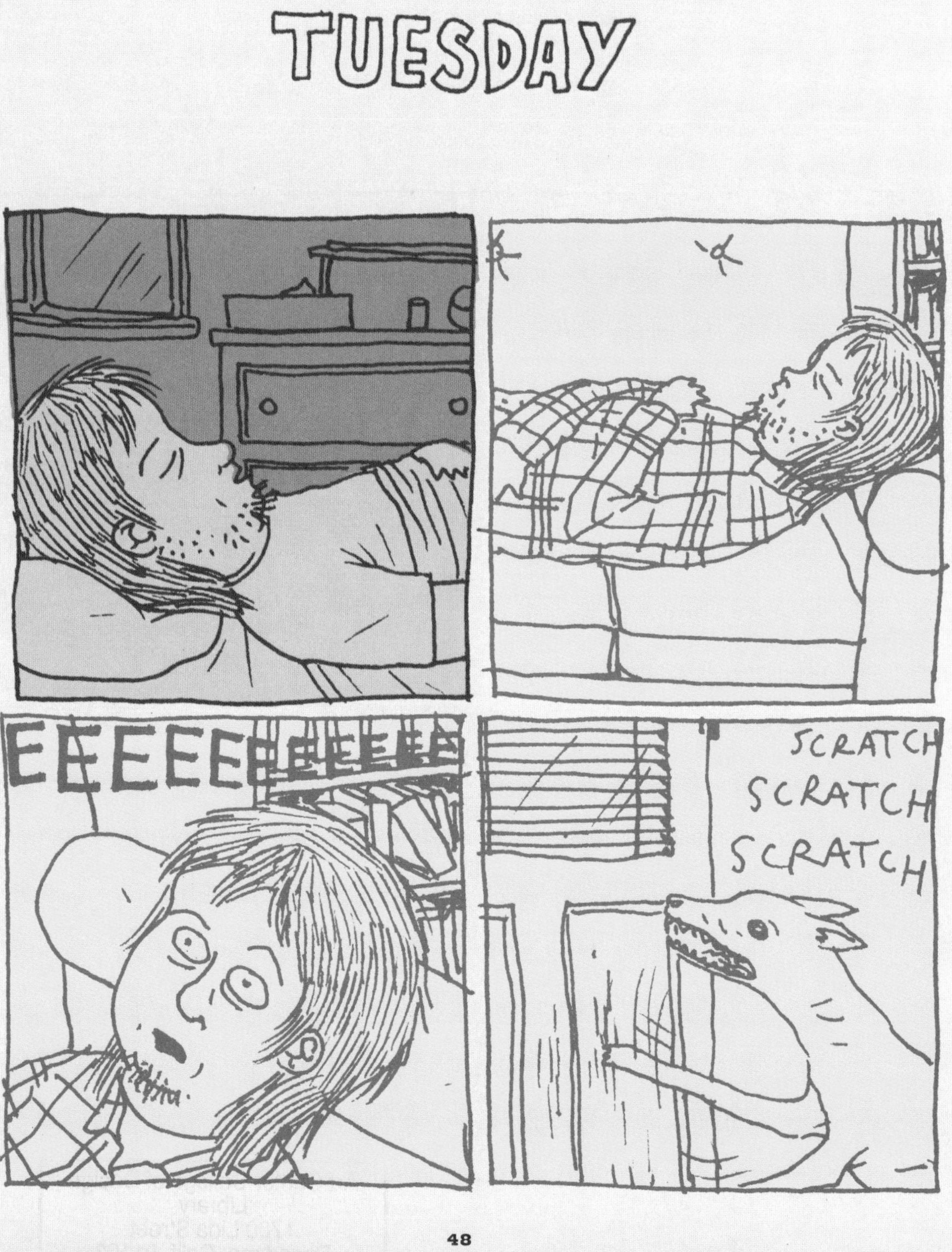
EEEEEEEEEEEE
SCRATCH
SCRATCH
SCRATCH

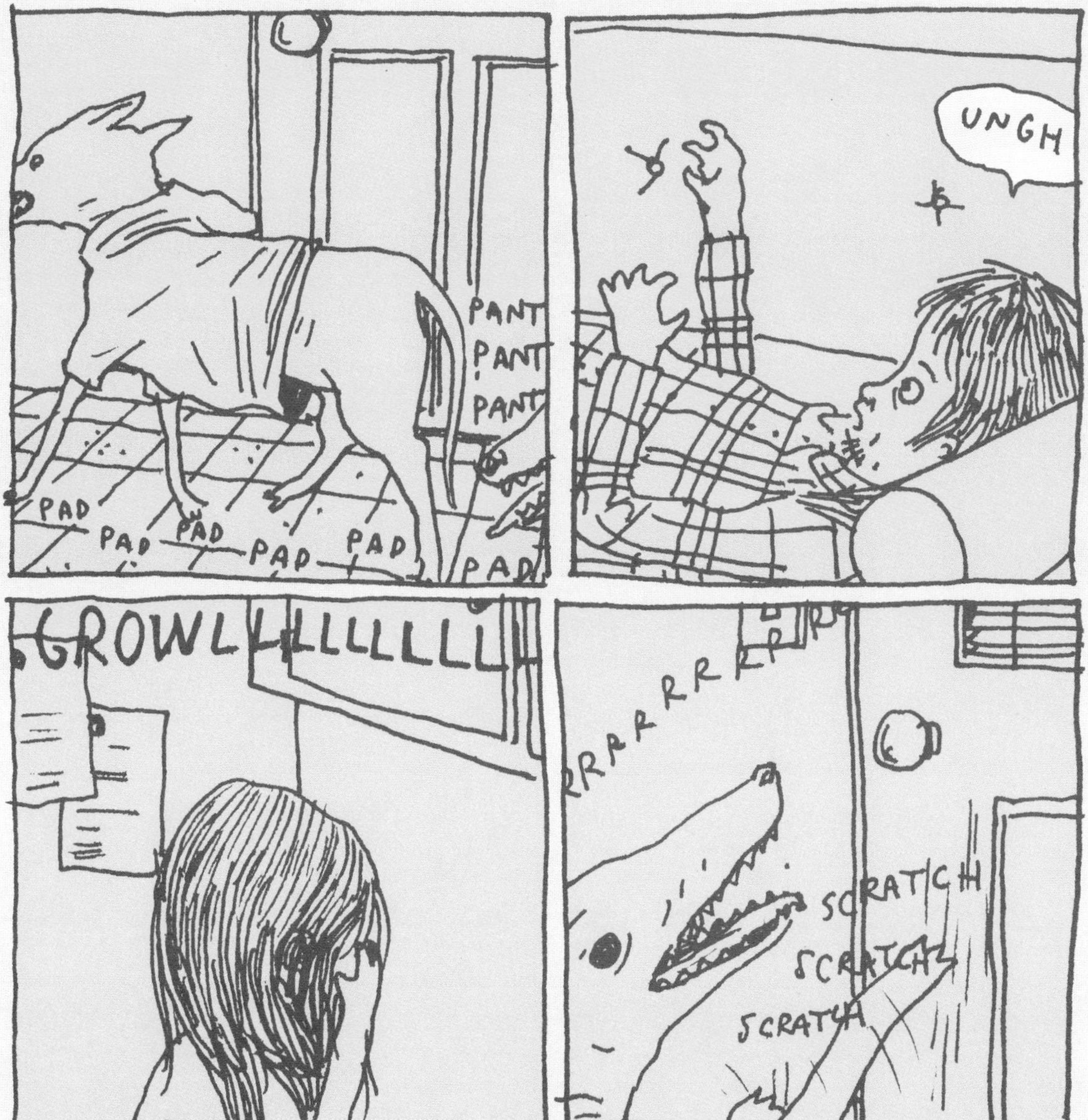
PANT
PANT
PANT
PAD PAD PAD PAD PAD PAD
UNGH
GROWLLLLLLLLLL
RRRRRRRRRR
SCRATCH
SCRATCH
SCRATCH

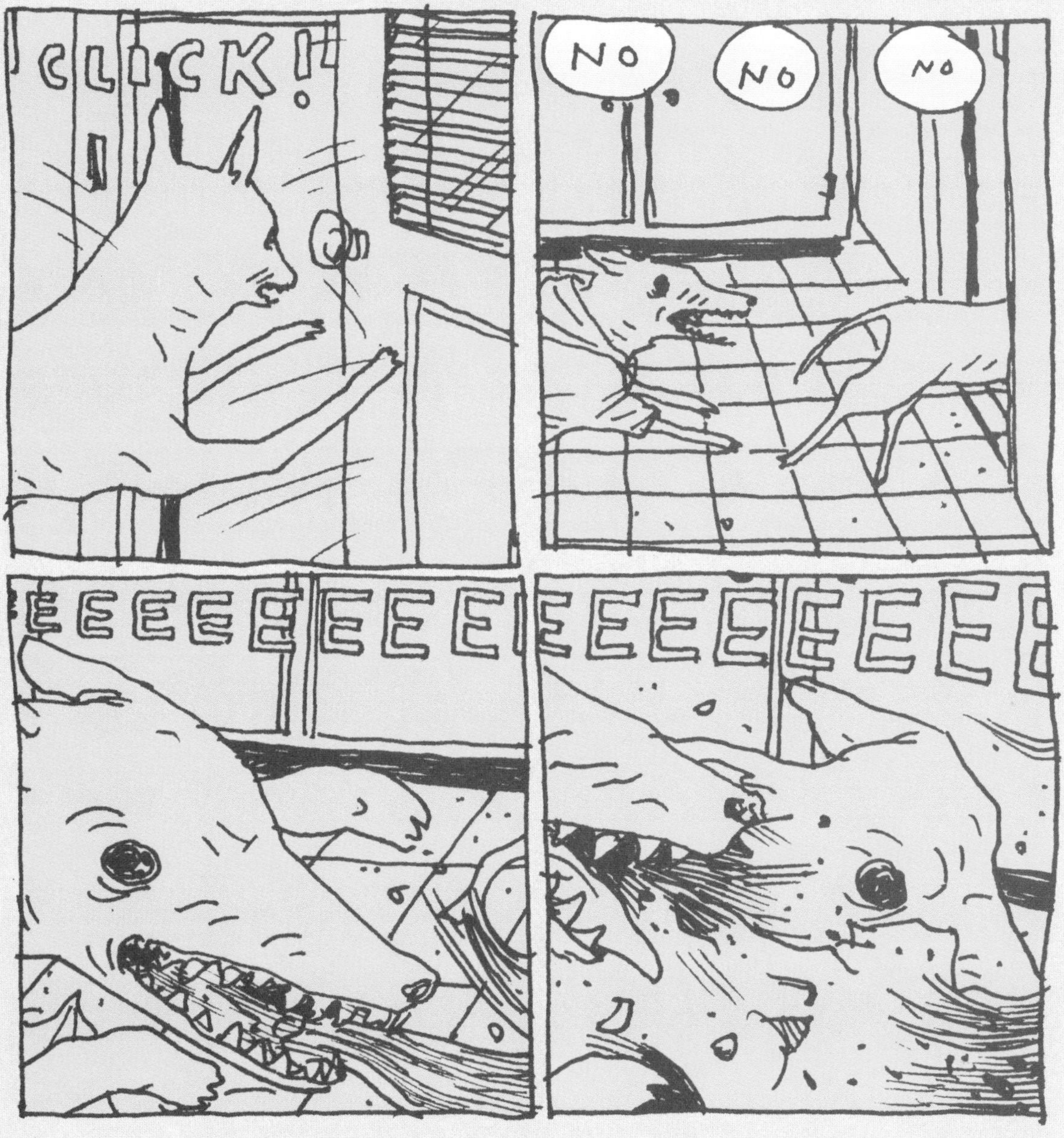
CLICK!
NO
NO
NO
EEEEEEEEEEEEEEEEEEEEEEEEEEE

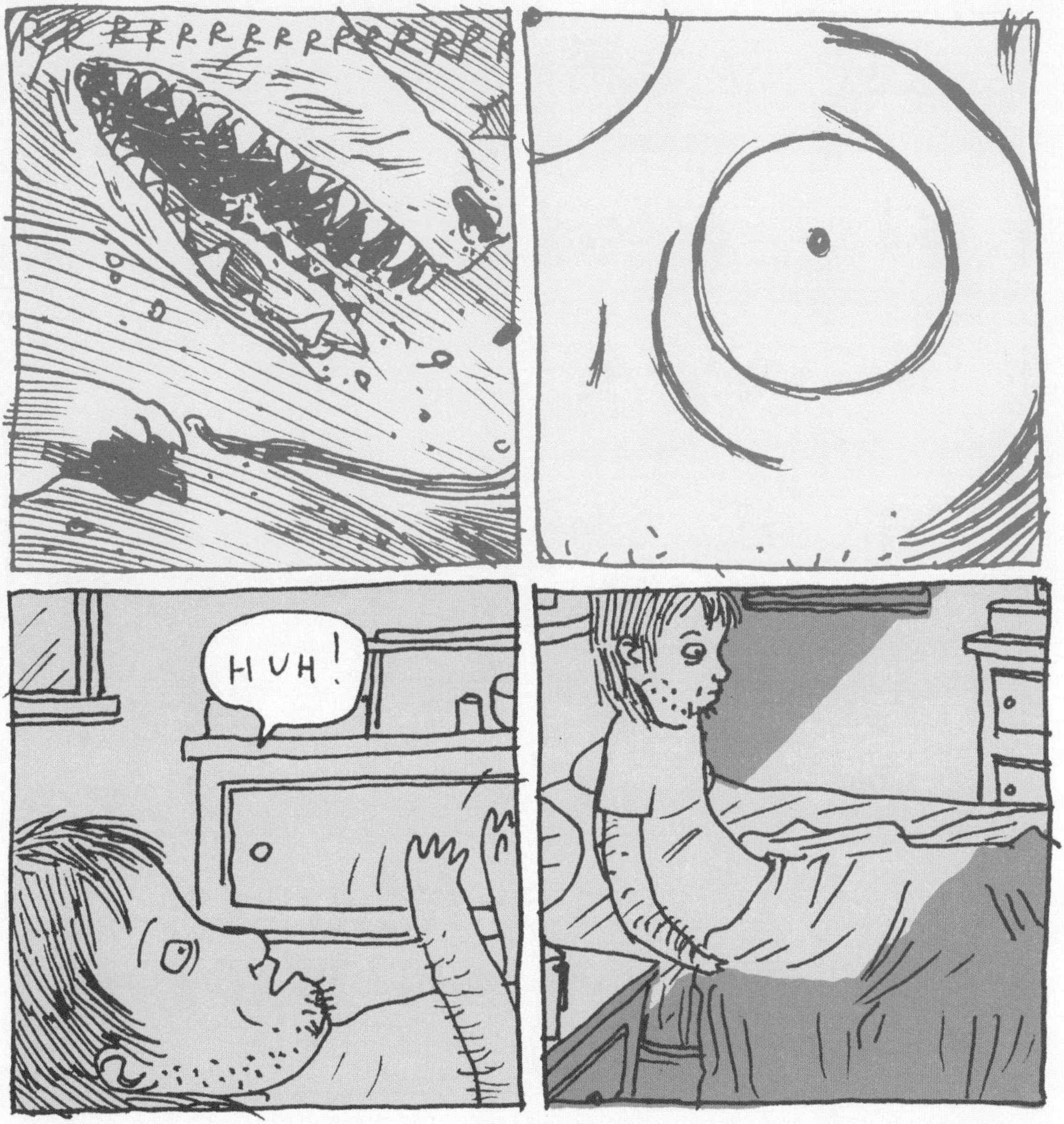
RRRRRRRRRRRRRRRRR
HUH!

WEDNESDAY MORNING

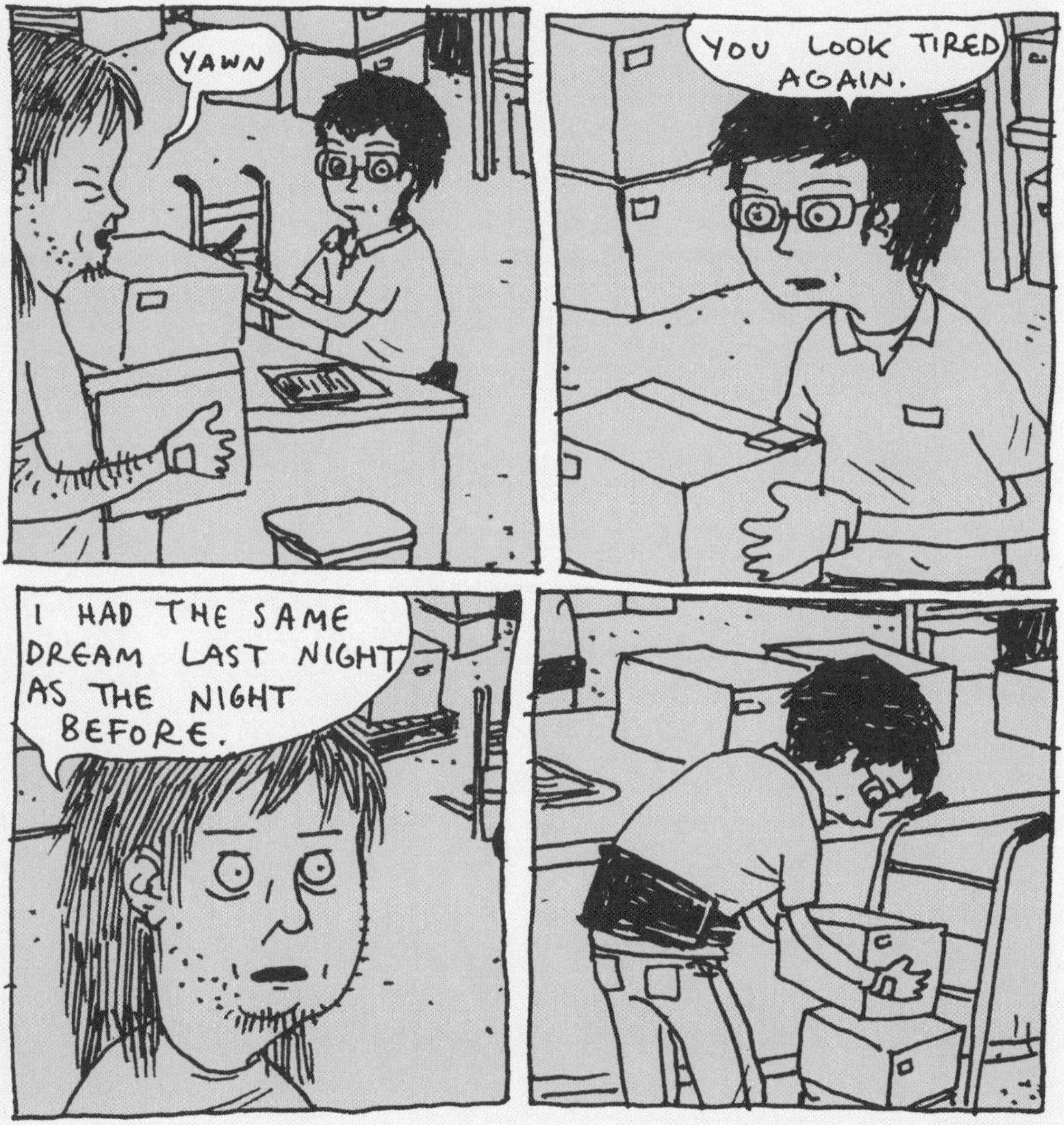

YAWN
YOU LOOK TIRED AGAIN.
I HAD THE SAME DREAM LAST NIGHT AS THE NIGHT BEFORE.

TRUCK BACKING UP!

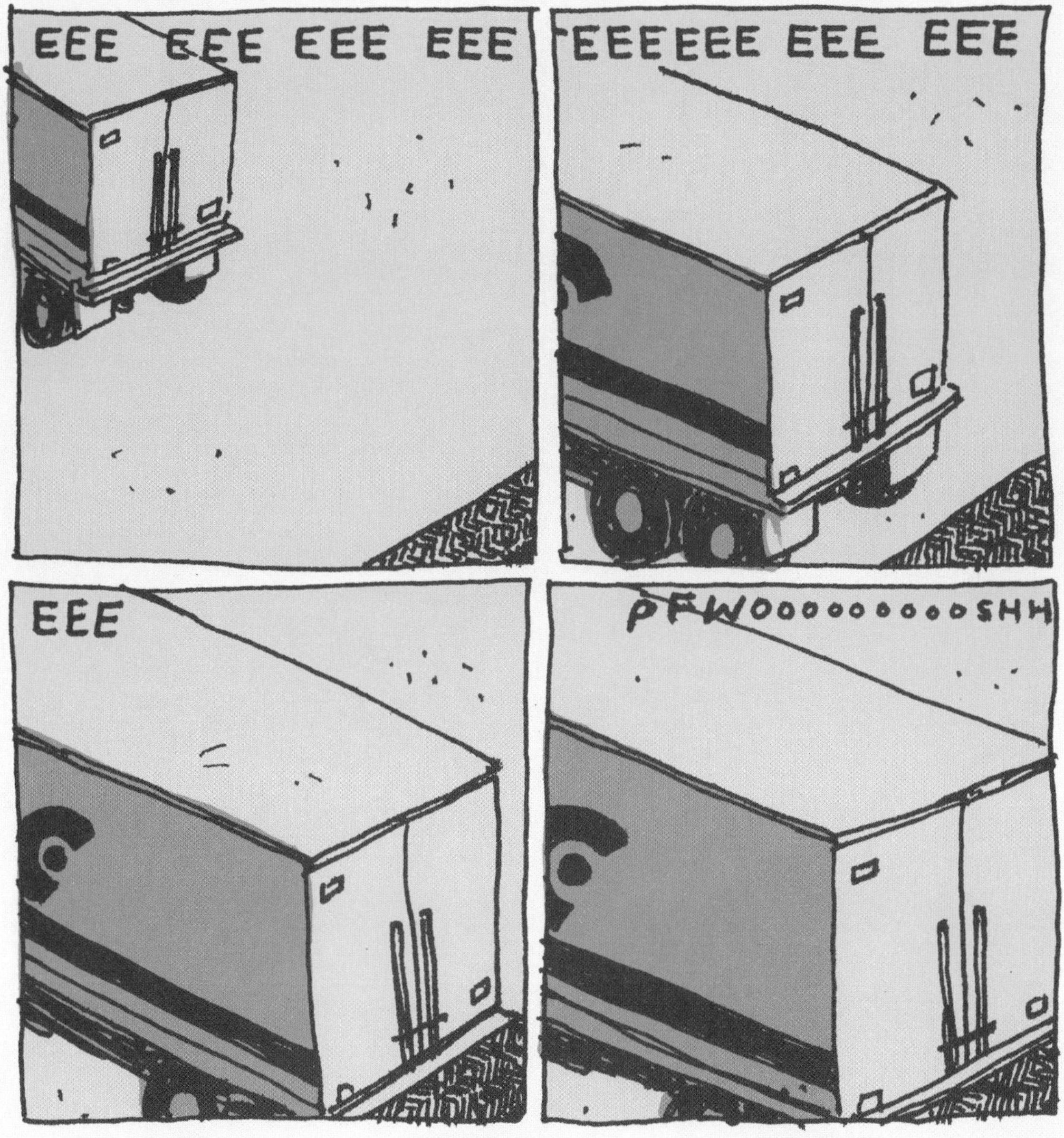
EEE EEE EEE EEE
EEEEEEE EEE EEE
EEE
PFWOOOOOOOOOSHH

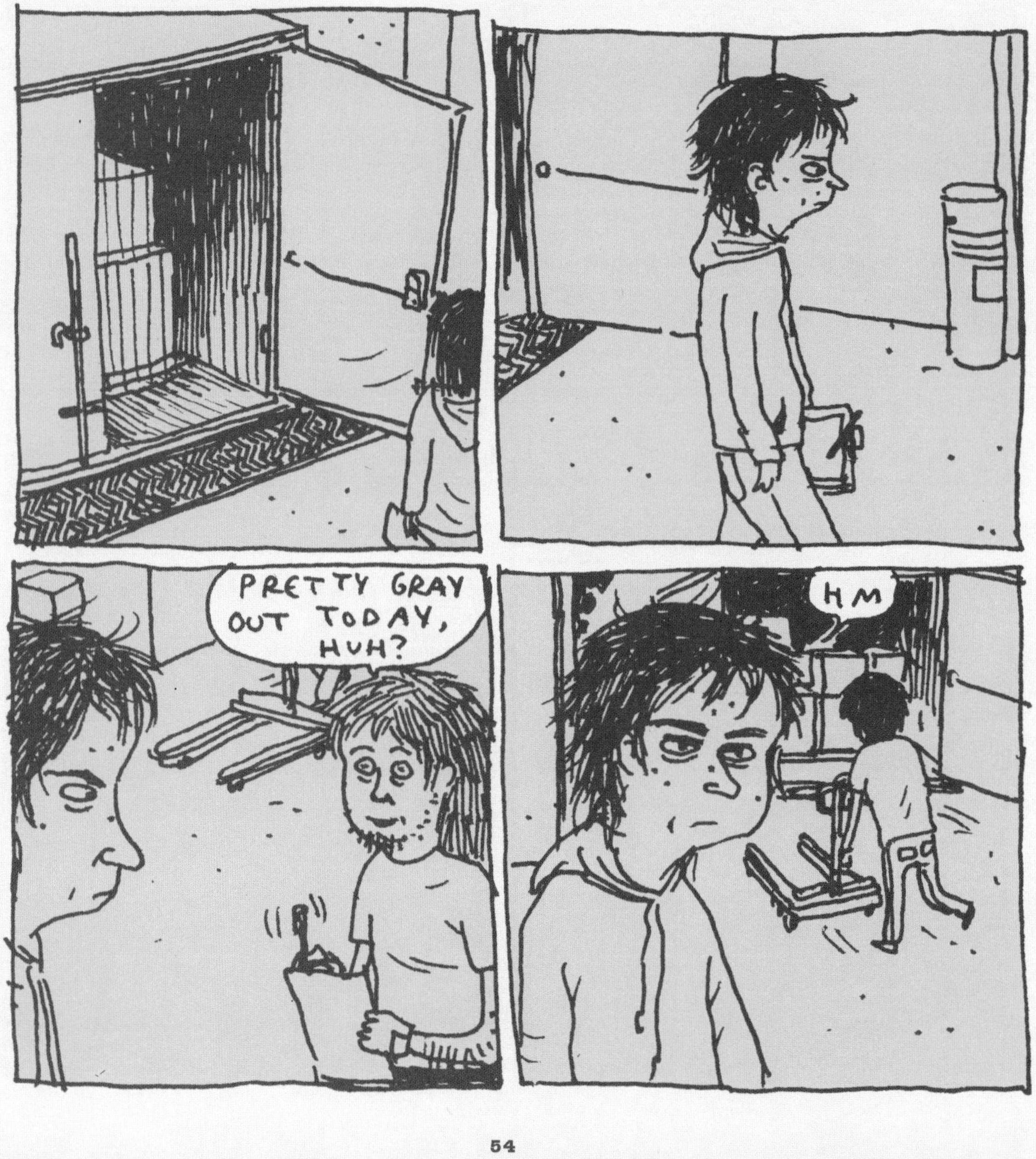
PRETTY GRAY OUT TODAY, HUH?
HM

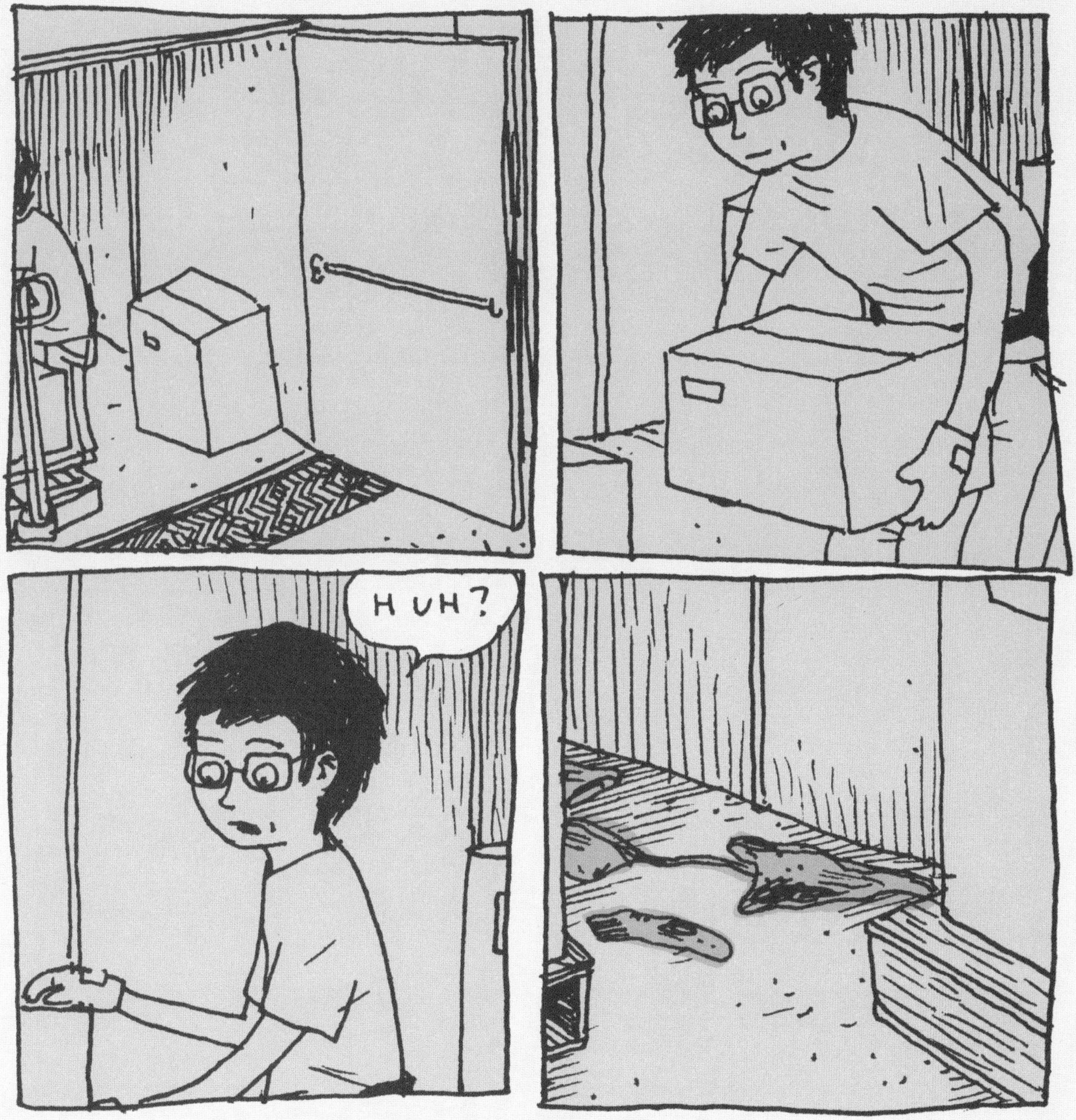
HUH?

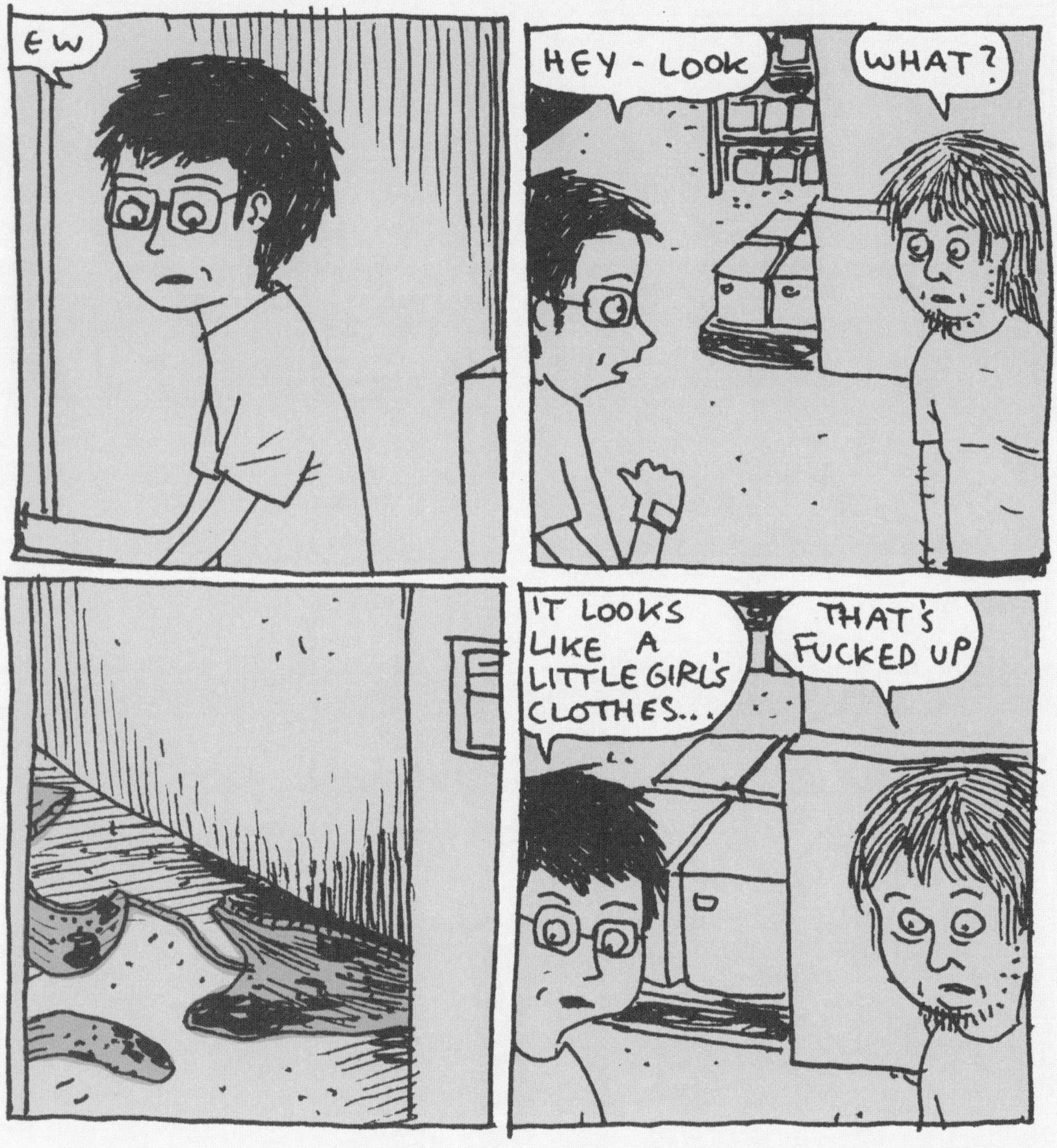
EW
HEY - LOOK
WHAT?
IT LOOKS LIKE A LITTLE GIRL'S CLOTHES...
THAT'S FUCKED UP

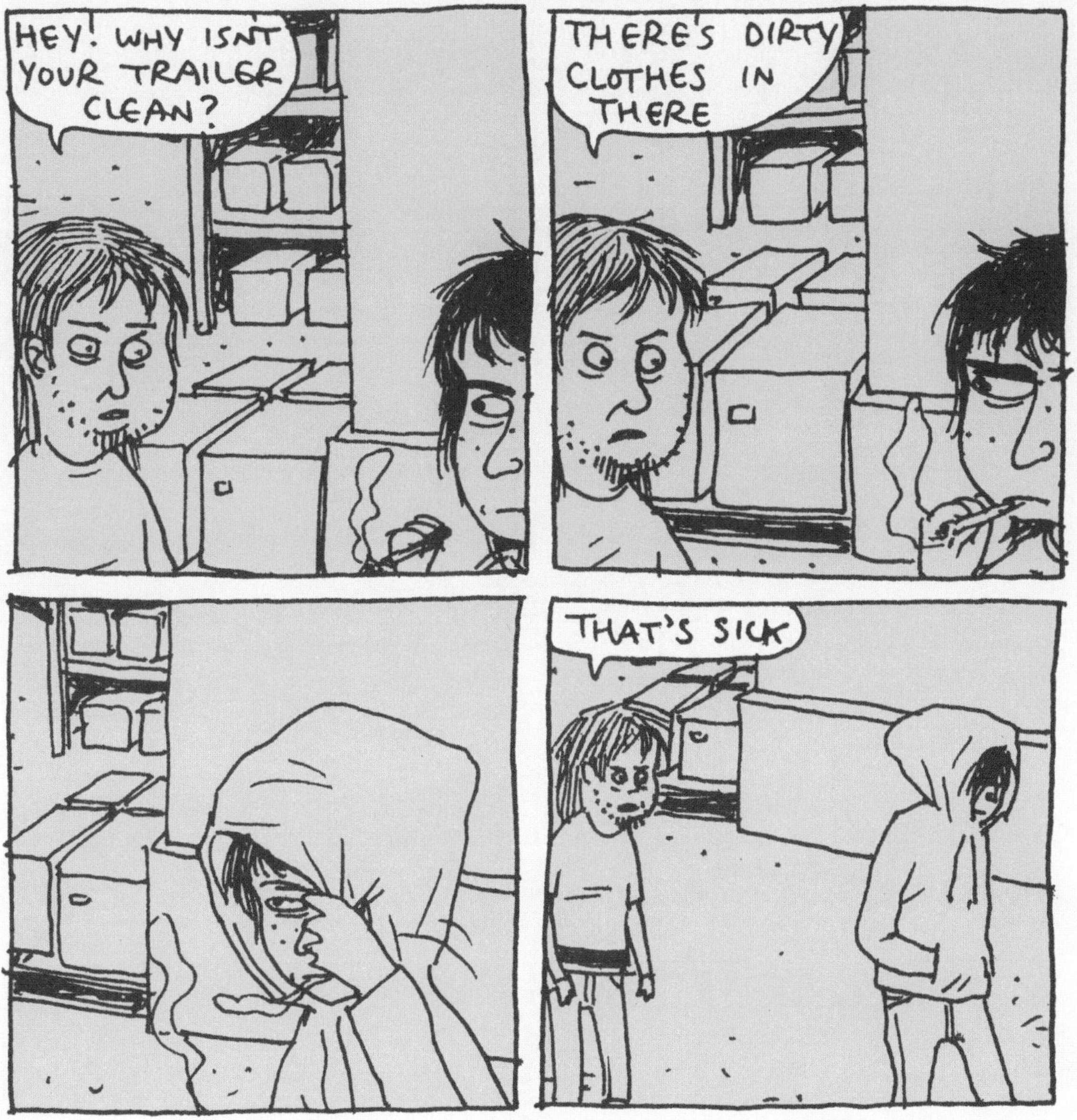
HEY! WHY ISNT YOUR TRAILER CLEAN?
THERE'S DIRTY CLOTHES IN THERE
THAT'S SICK

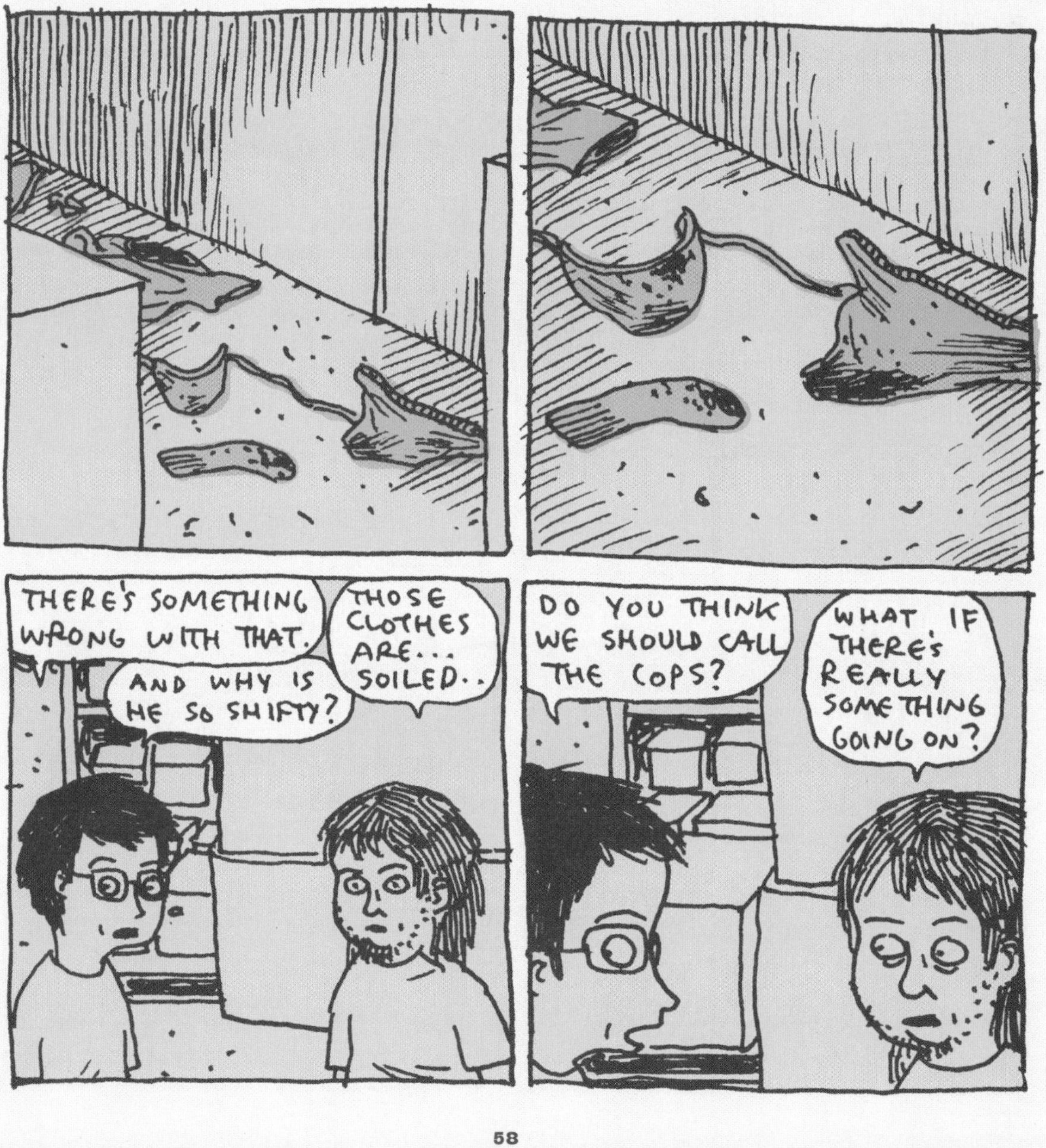
THERE'S SOMETHING WRONG WITH THAT.
THOSE CLOTHES ARE... SOILED..
AND WHY IS HE SO SHIFTY?
DO YOU THINK WE SHOULD CALL THE COPS?
WHAT IF THERE'S REALLY SOMETHING GOING ON?

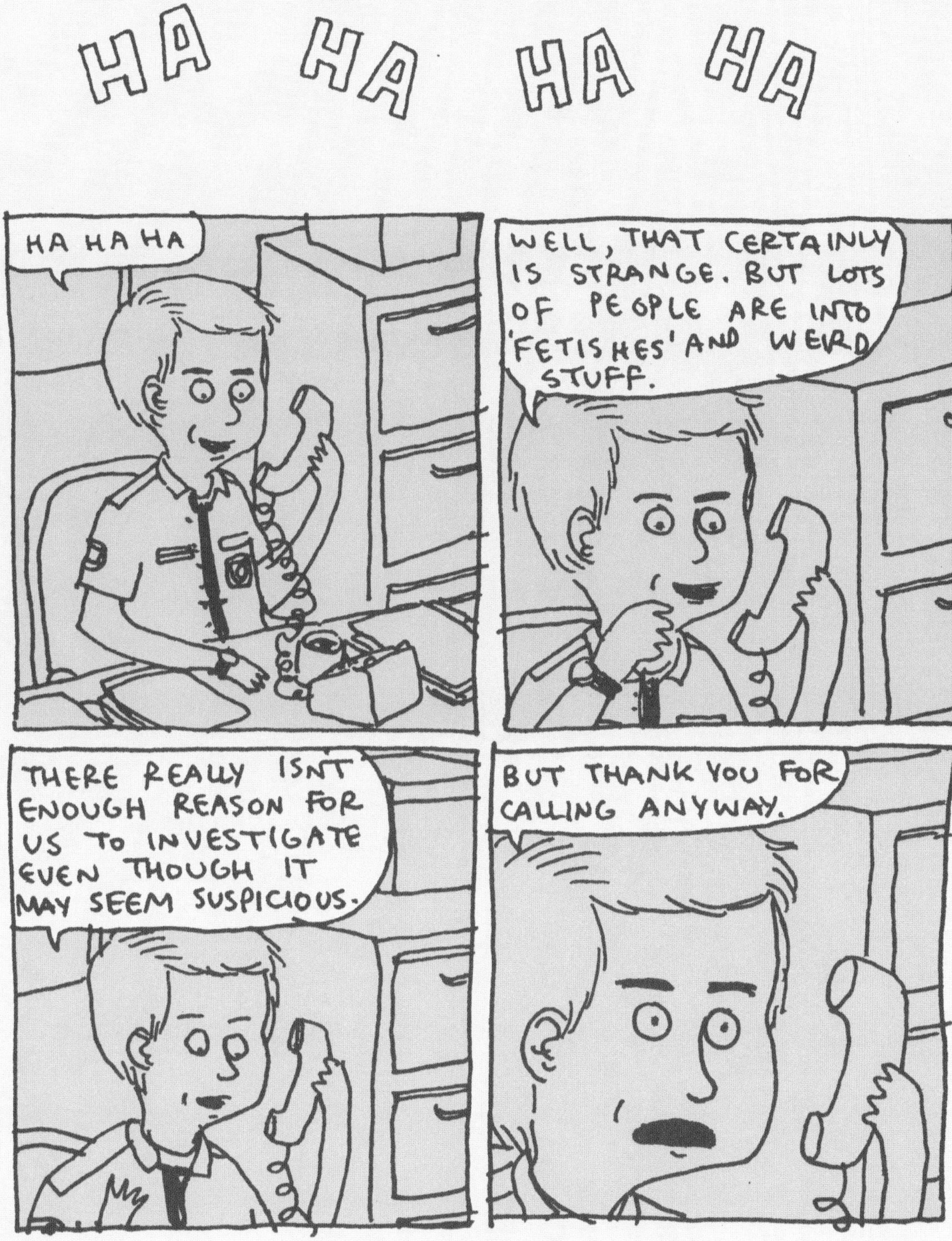
HA HA HA HA
HA HA HA
WELL, THAT CERTAINLY IS STRANGE. BUT LOTS OF PEOPLE ARE INTO 'FETISHES' AND WEIRD STUFF.
THERE REALLY ISNT ENOUGH REASON FOR US TO INVESTIGATE EVEN THOUGH IT MAY SEEM SUSPICIOUS.
BUT THANK YOU FOR CALLING ANYWAY.

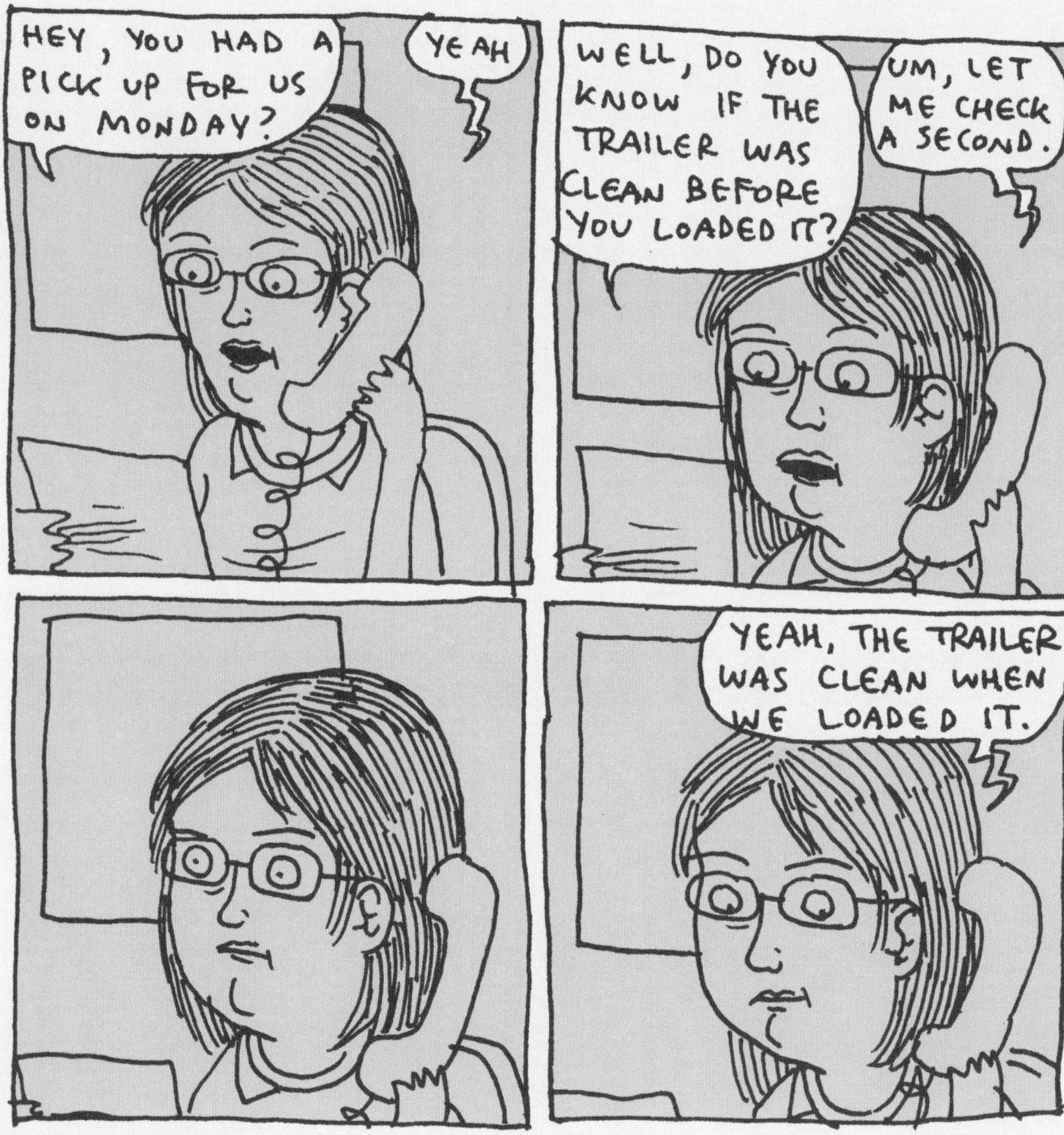
HEY, YOU HAD A PICK UP FOR US ON MONDAY?
YEAH
WELL, DO YOU KNOW IF THE TRAILER WAS CLEAN BEFORE YOU LOADED IT?
UM, LET ME CHECK A SECOND.
YEAH, THE TRAILER WAS CLEAN WHEN WE LOADED IT.

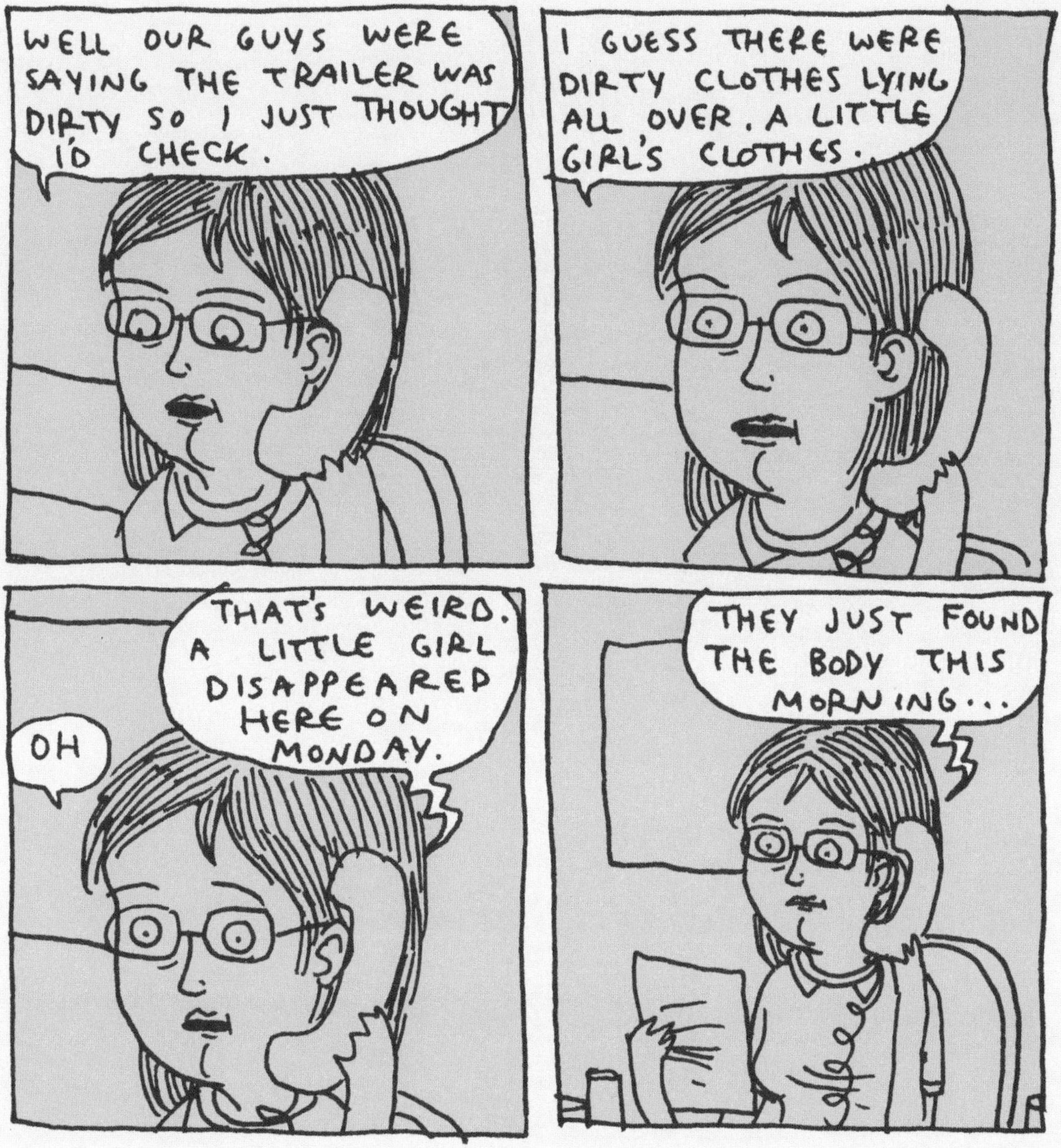
WELL OUR GUYS WERE SAYING THE TRAILER WAS DIRTY SO I JUST THOUGHT I'D CHECK.
I GUESS THERE WERE DIRTY CLOTHES LYING ALL OVER. A LITTLE GIRL'S CLOTHES.
THAT'S WEIRD. A LITTLE GIRL DISAPPEARED HERE ON MONDAY.
OH
THEY JUST FOUND THE BODY THIS MORNING...

COPS

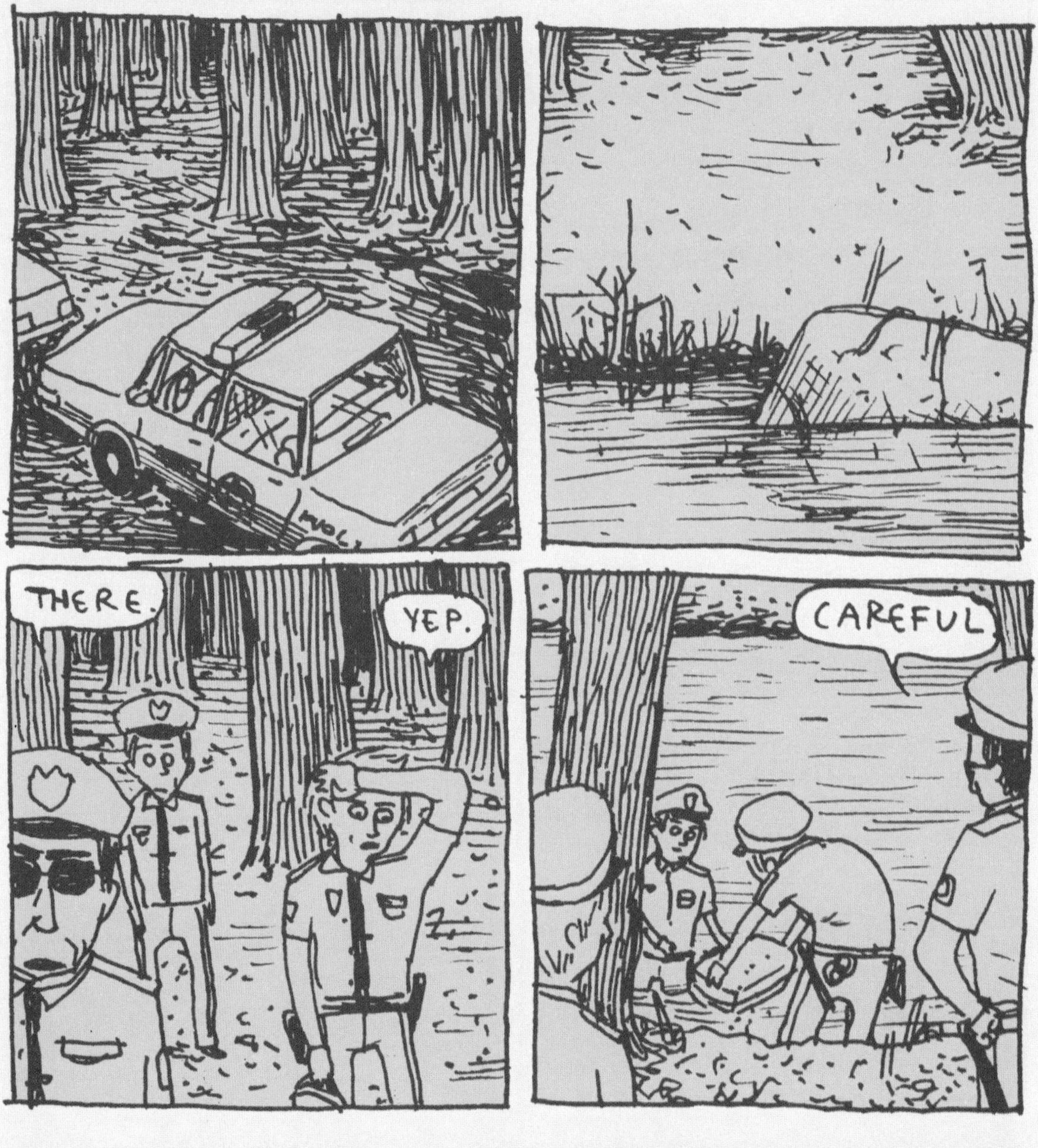
THERE.
YEP.
CAREFUL

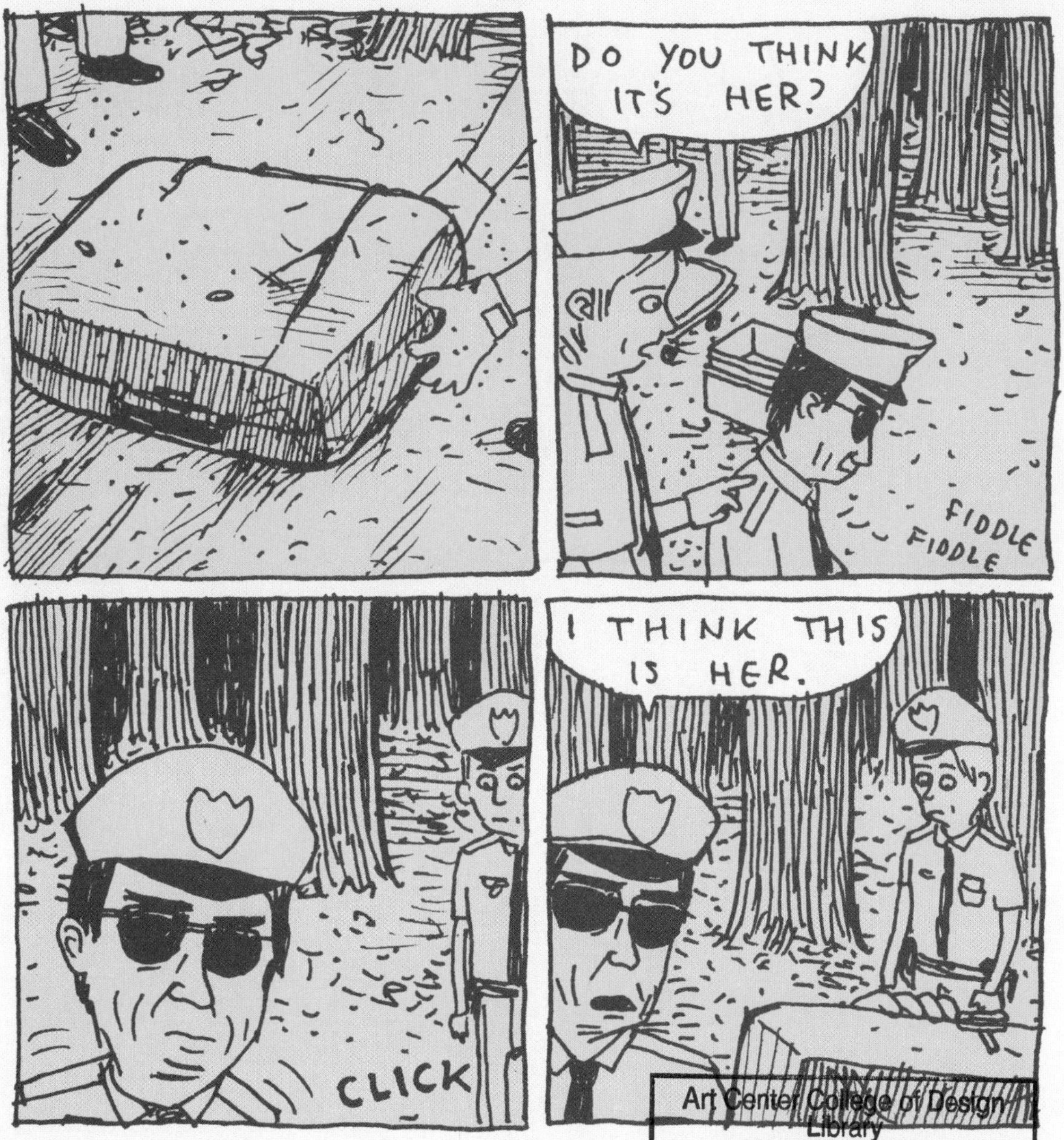
DO YOU THINK IT'S HER?
FIDDLE FIDDLE
CLICK
I THINK THIS IS HER.

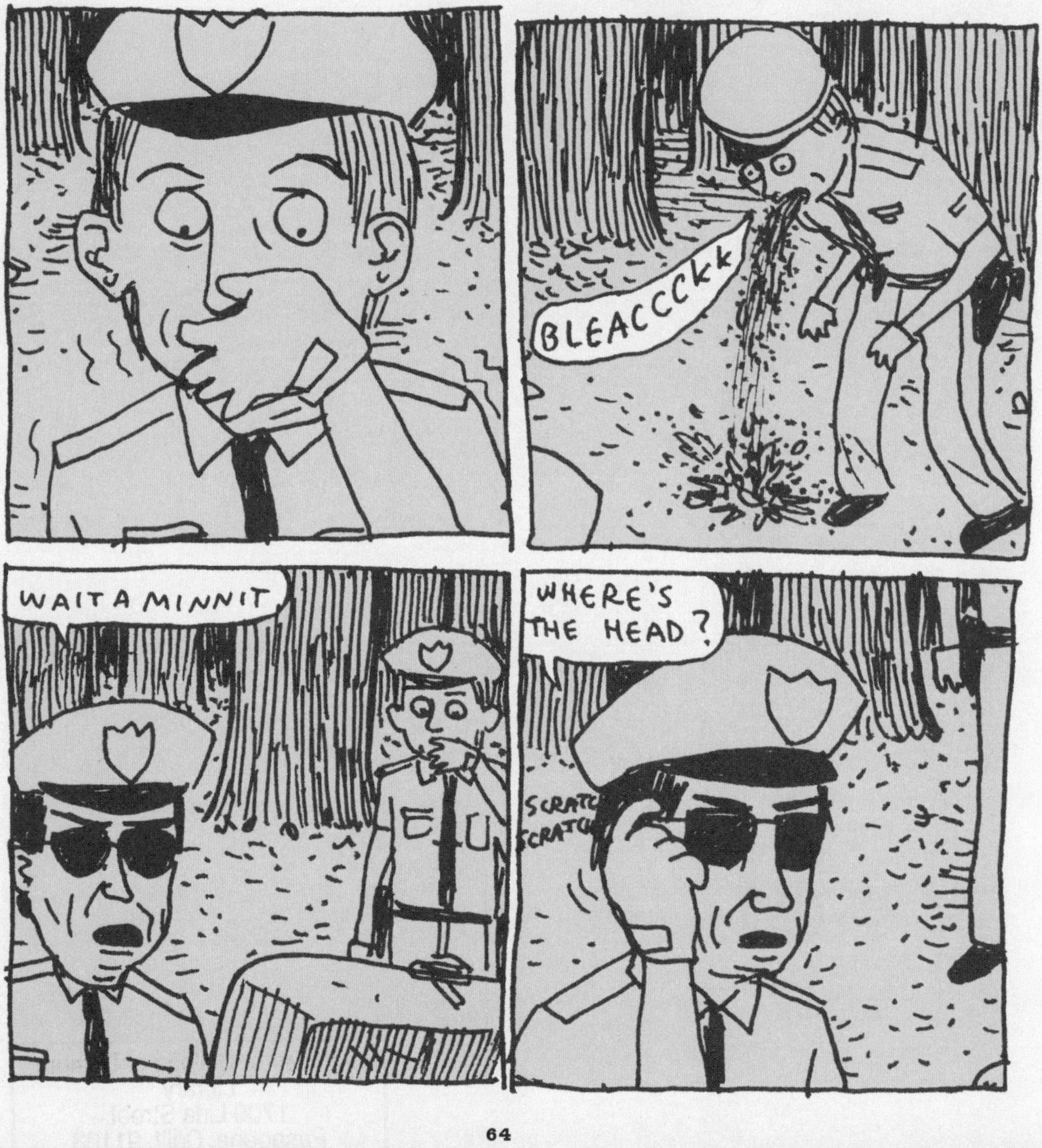
BLEACCCCKk
WAITAMINNIT
WHERE'S THE HEAD?
SCRATC
SCRATC

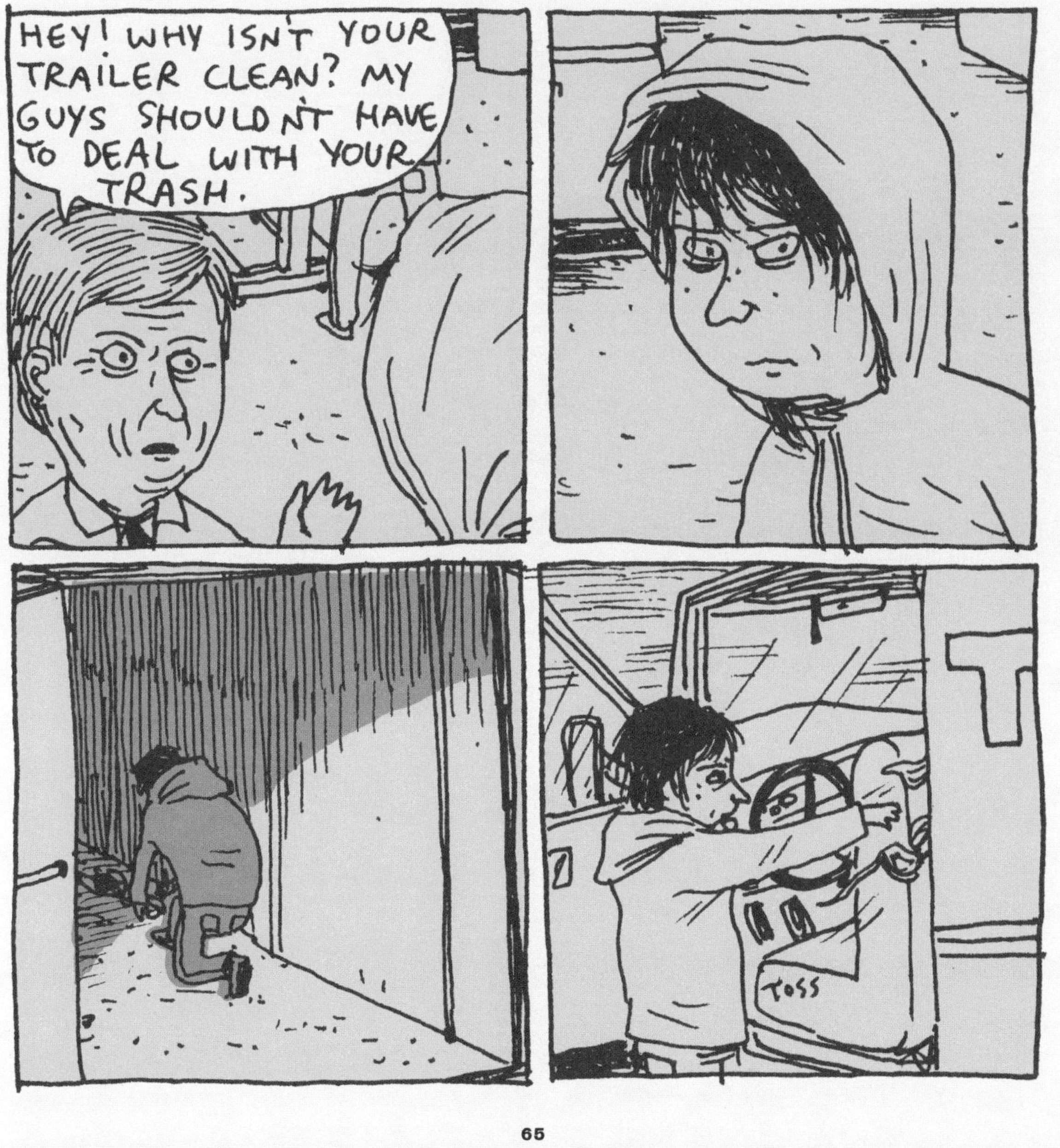
HEY! WHY ISN'T YOUR TRAILER CLEAN? MY GUYS SHOULDN'T HAVE TO DEAL WITH YOUR TRASH.
TOSS

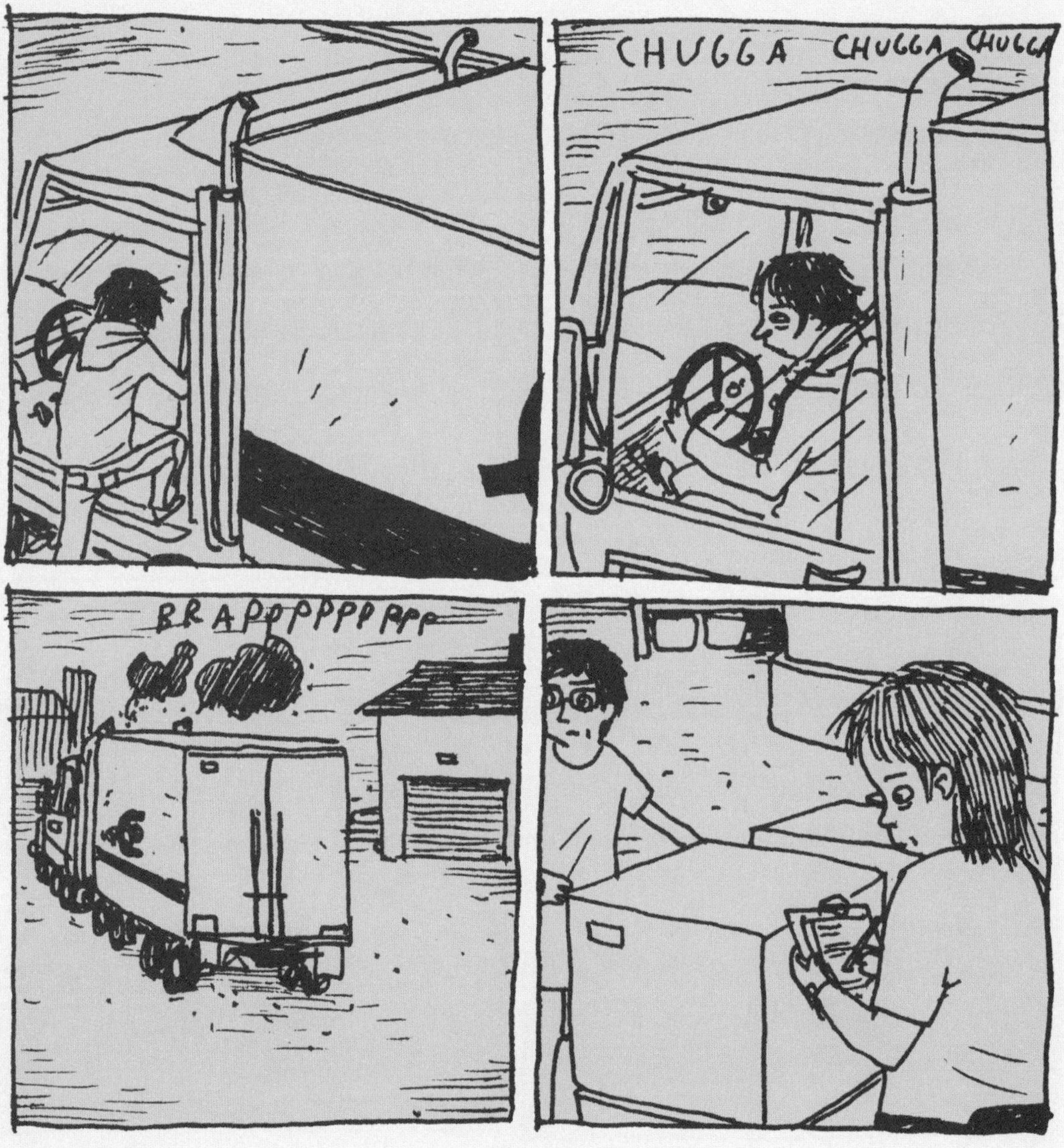
CHUGGA CHUGGA CHUGGA
BRAPPPPPPPPP

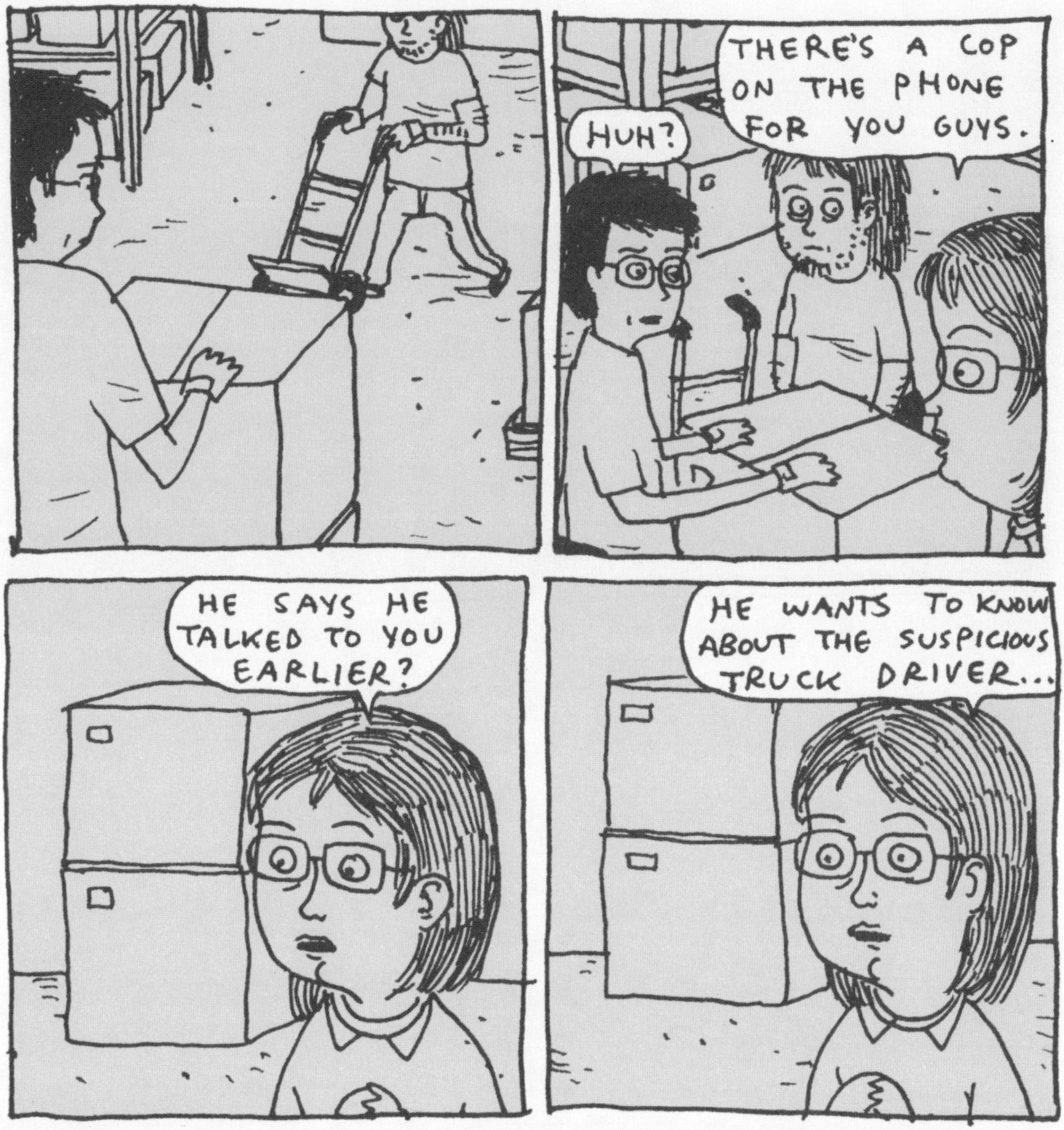
HUH?
THERE'S A COP ON THE PHONE FOR YOU GUYS.
HE SAYS HE TALKED TO YOU EARLIER?
HE WANTS TO KNOW ABOUT THE SUSPICIOUS TRUCK DRIVER...

happy BIRTHDAY

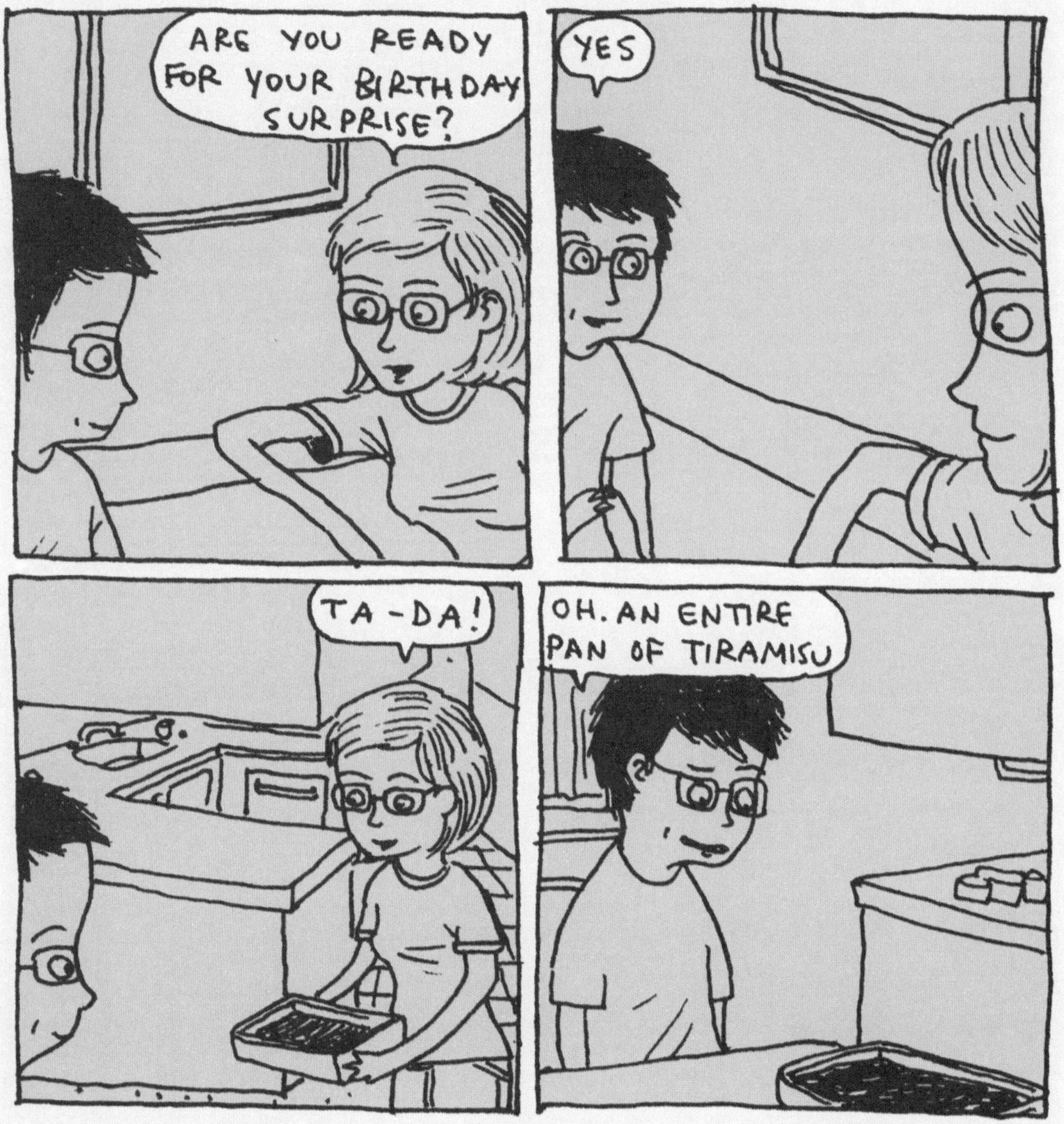
ARE YOU READY FOR YOUR BIRTHDAY SURPRISE?
YES
TA-DA!
OH. AN ENTIRE PAN OF TIRAMISU

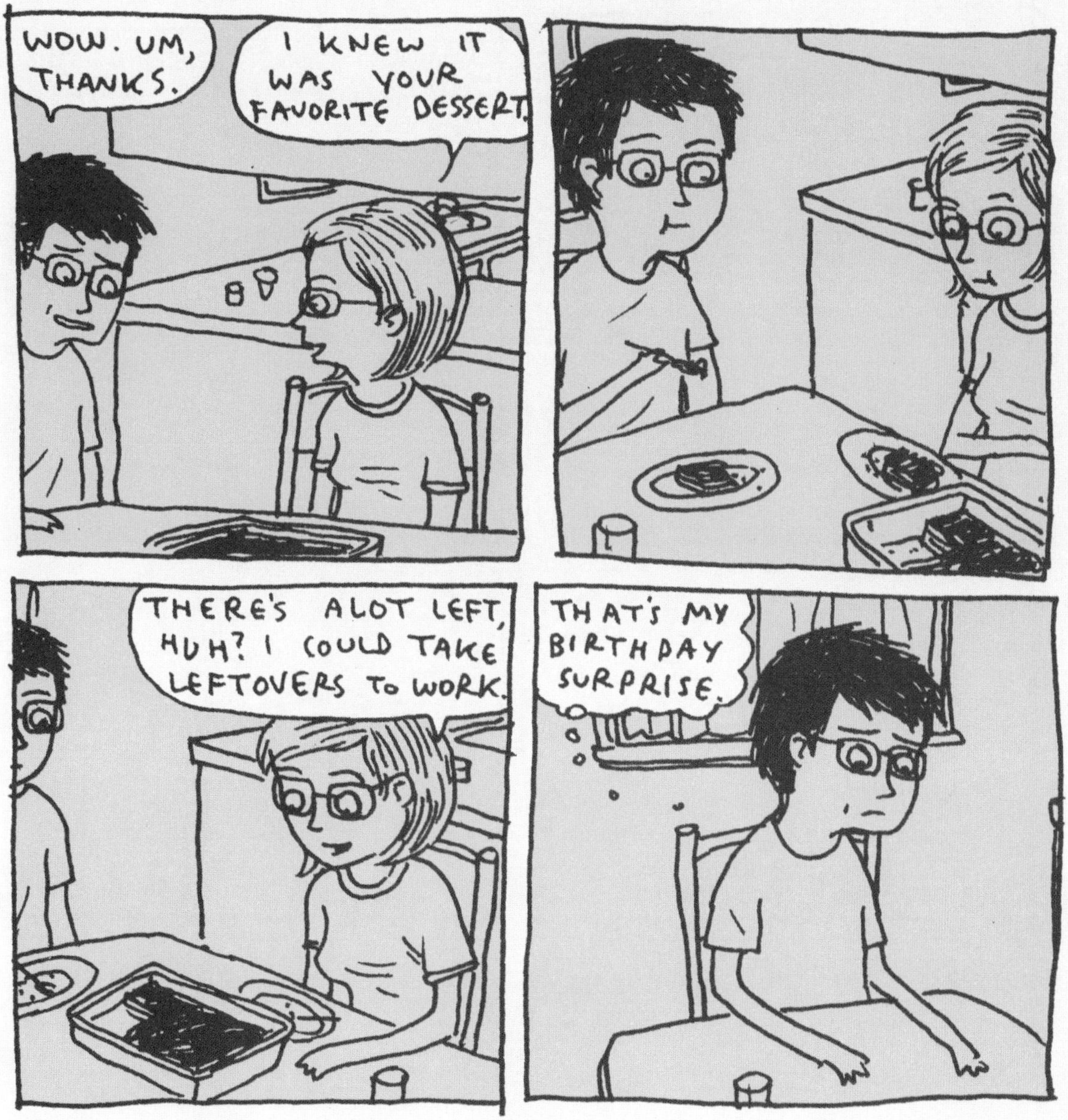
WOW. UM, THANKS.
I KNEW IT WAS YOUR FAVORITE DESSERT.
THERE'S ALOT LEFT, HUH? I COULD TAKE LEFTOVERS TO WORK.
THAT'S MY BIRTHDAY SURPRISE.

THURSDAY

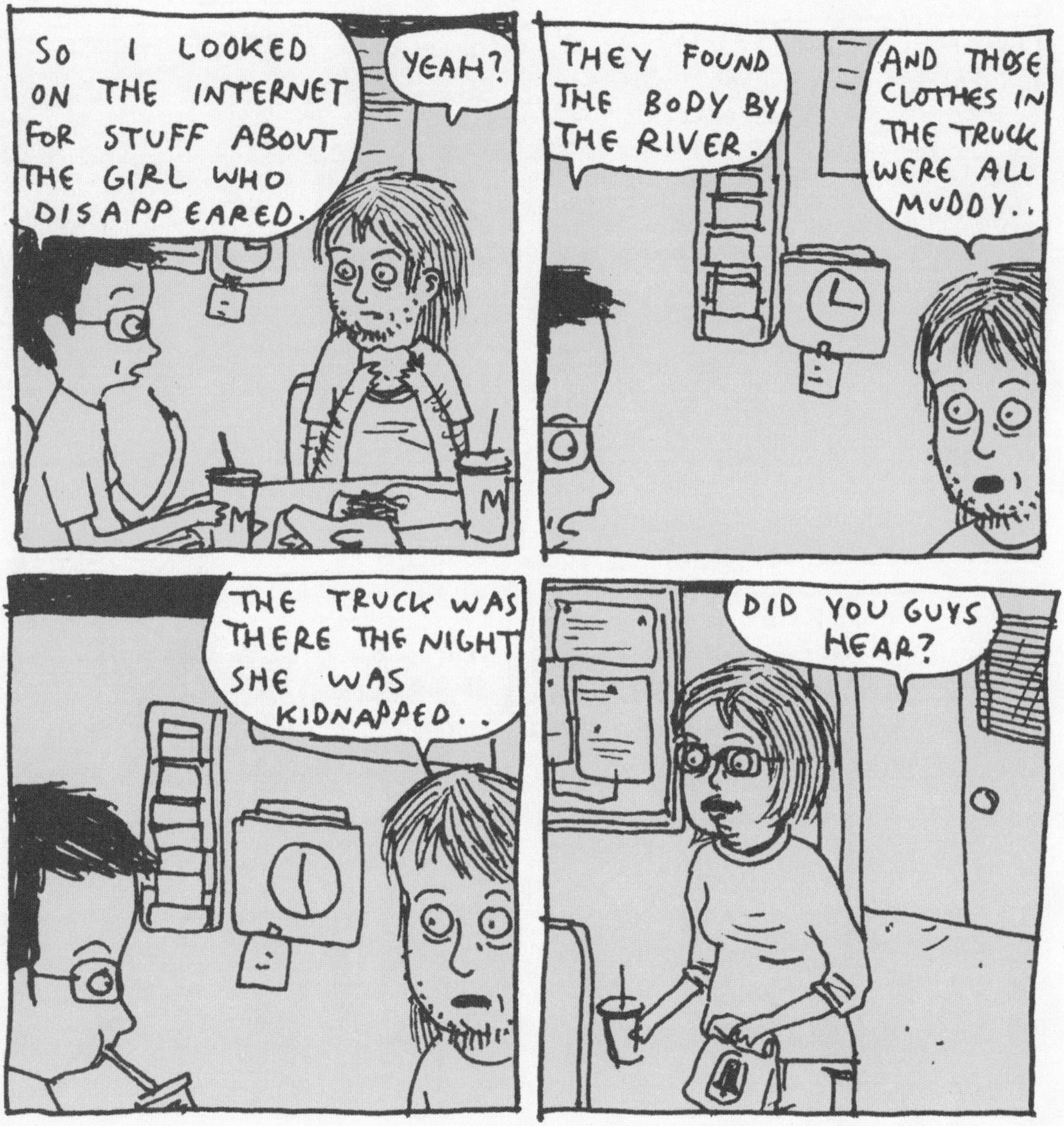
SO I LOOKED ON THE INTERNET FOR STUFF ABOUT THE GIRL WHO DISAPPEARED.
YEAH?
THEY FOUND THE BODY BY THE RIVER.
AND THOSE CLOTHES IN THE TRUCK WERE ALL MUDDY..
THE TRUCK WAS THERE THE NIGHT SHE WAS KIDNAPPED..
DID YOU GUYS HEAR?

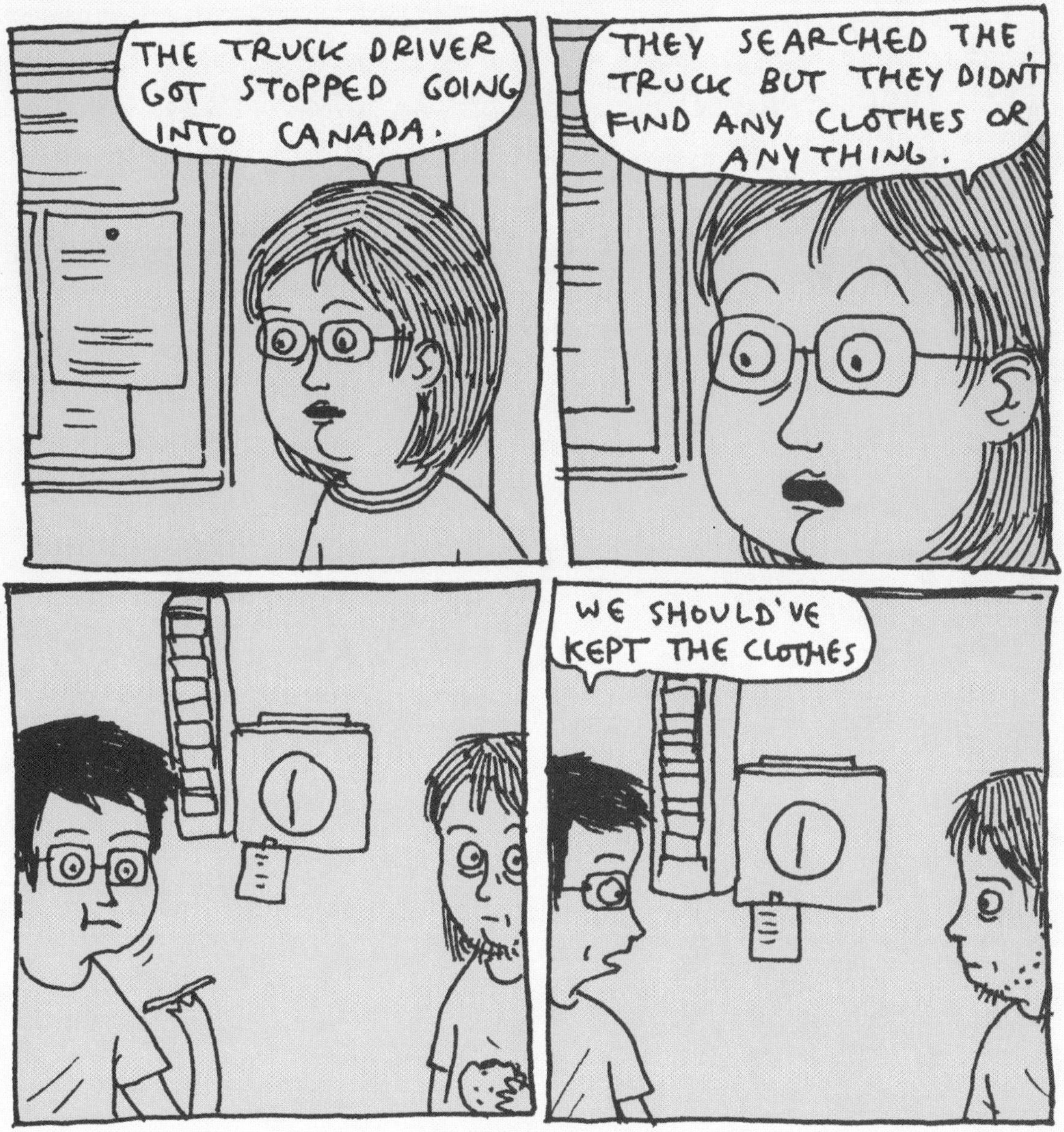
THE TRUCK DRIVER GOT STOPPED GOING INTO CANADA.
THEY SEARCHED THE TRUCK BUT THEY DIDN'T FIND ANY CLOTHES OR ANYTHING.
WE SHOULD'VE KEPT THE CLOTHES

PSYCHIC MOM

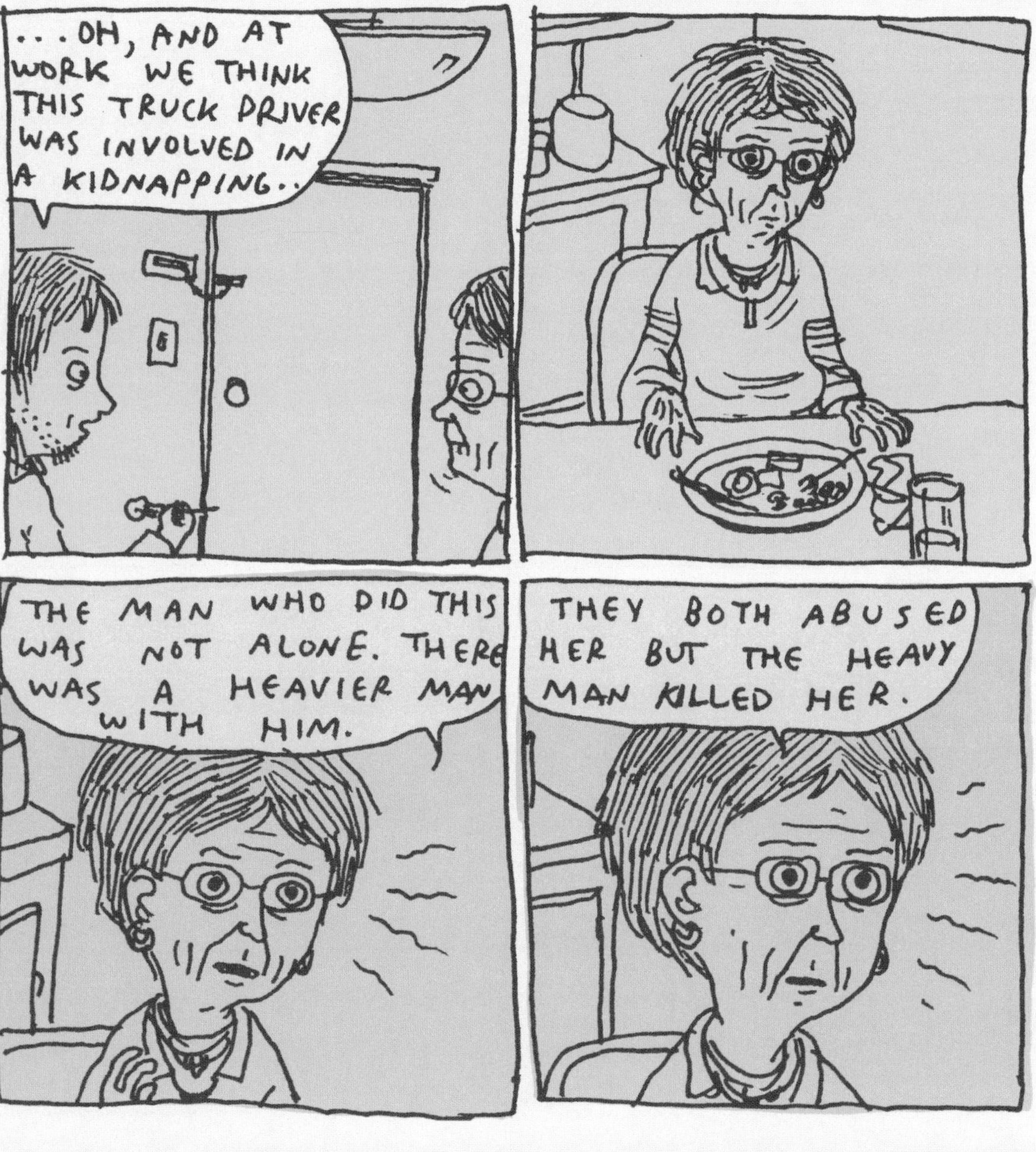

...OH, AND AT WORK WE THINK THIS TRUCK DRIVER WAS INVOLVED IN A KIDNAPPING...
THE MAN WHO DID THIS WAS NOT ALONE. THERE WAS A HEAVIER MAN WITH HIM.
THEY BOTH ABUSED HER BUT THE HEAVY MAN KILLED HER.

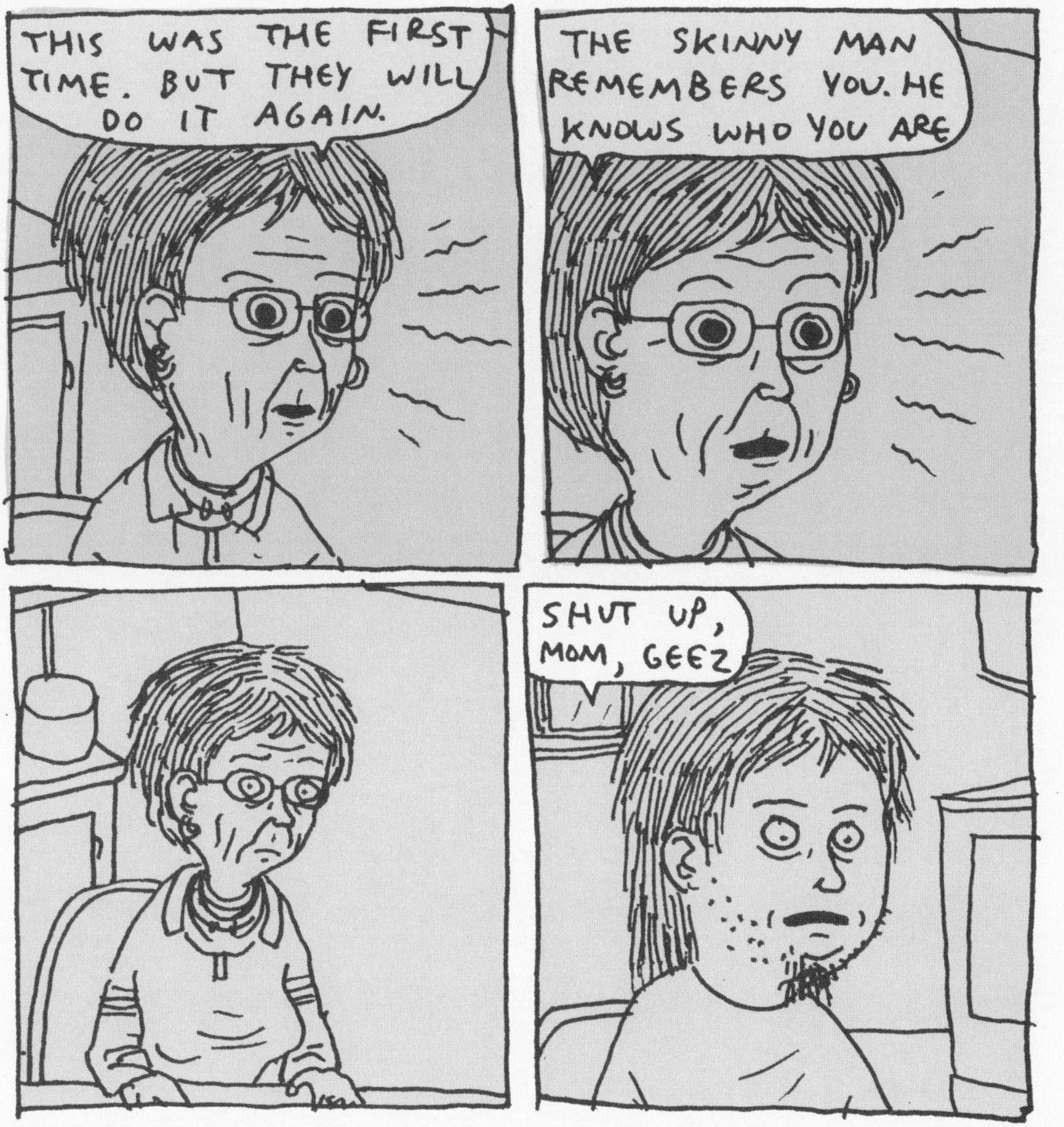
THIS WAS THE FIRST TIME. BUT THEY WILL DO IT AGAIN.
THE SKINNY MAN REMEMBERS YOU. HE KNOWS WHO YOU ARE
SHUT UP, MOM, GEEZ

EPILOGUE

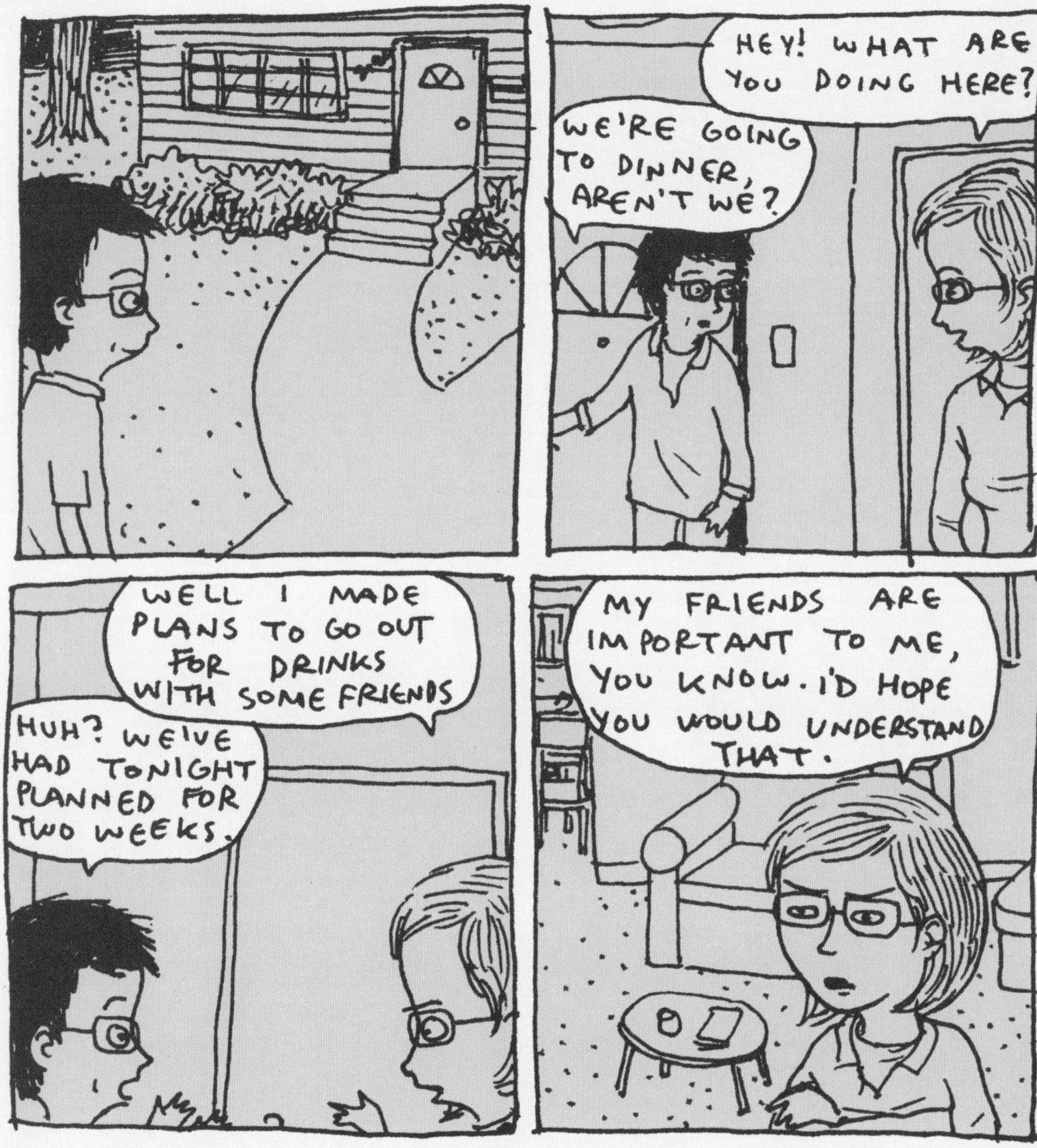
HEY! WHAT ARE YOU DOING HERE?
WE'RE GOING TO DINNER, AREN'T WE?
WELL I MADE PLANS TO GO OUT FOR DRINKS WITH SOME FRIENDS
HUH? WE'VE HAD TONIGHT PLANNED FOR TWO WEEKS.
MY FRIENDS ARE IMPORTANT TO ME, YOU KNOW. I'D HOPE YOU WOULD UNDERSTAND THAT.

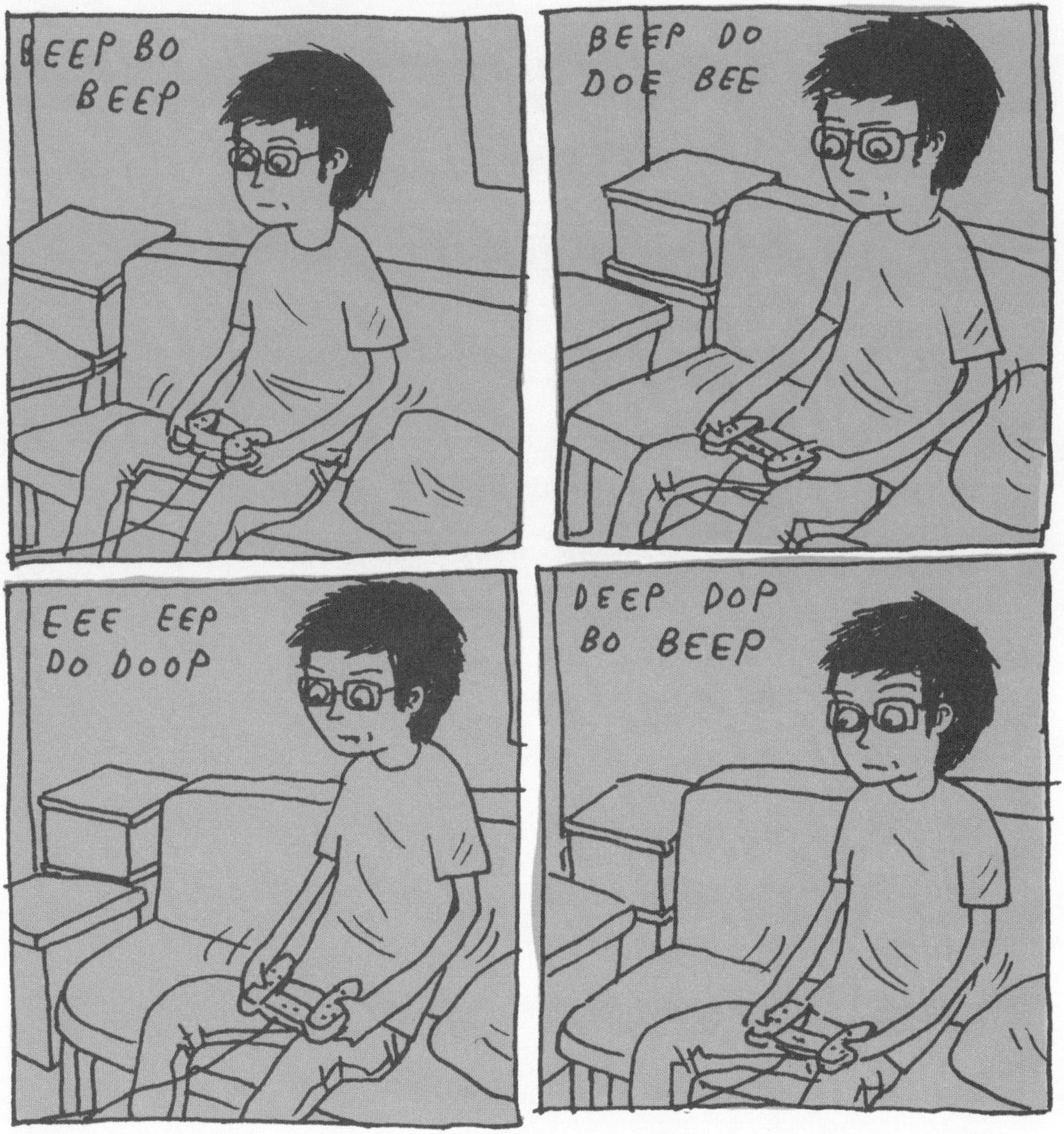
BEEP BO
BEEP
BEEP DO
DOE BEE
EEE EEP
DO DOOP
DEEP DOP
BO BEEP

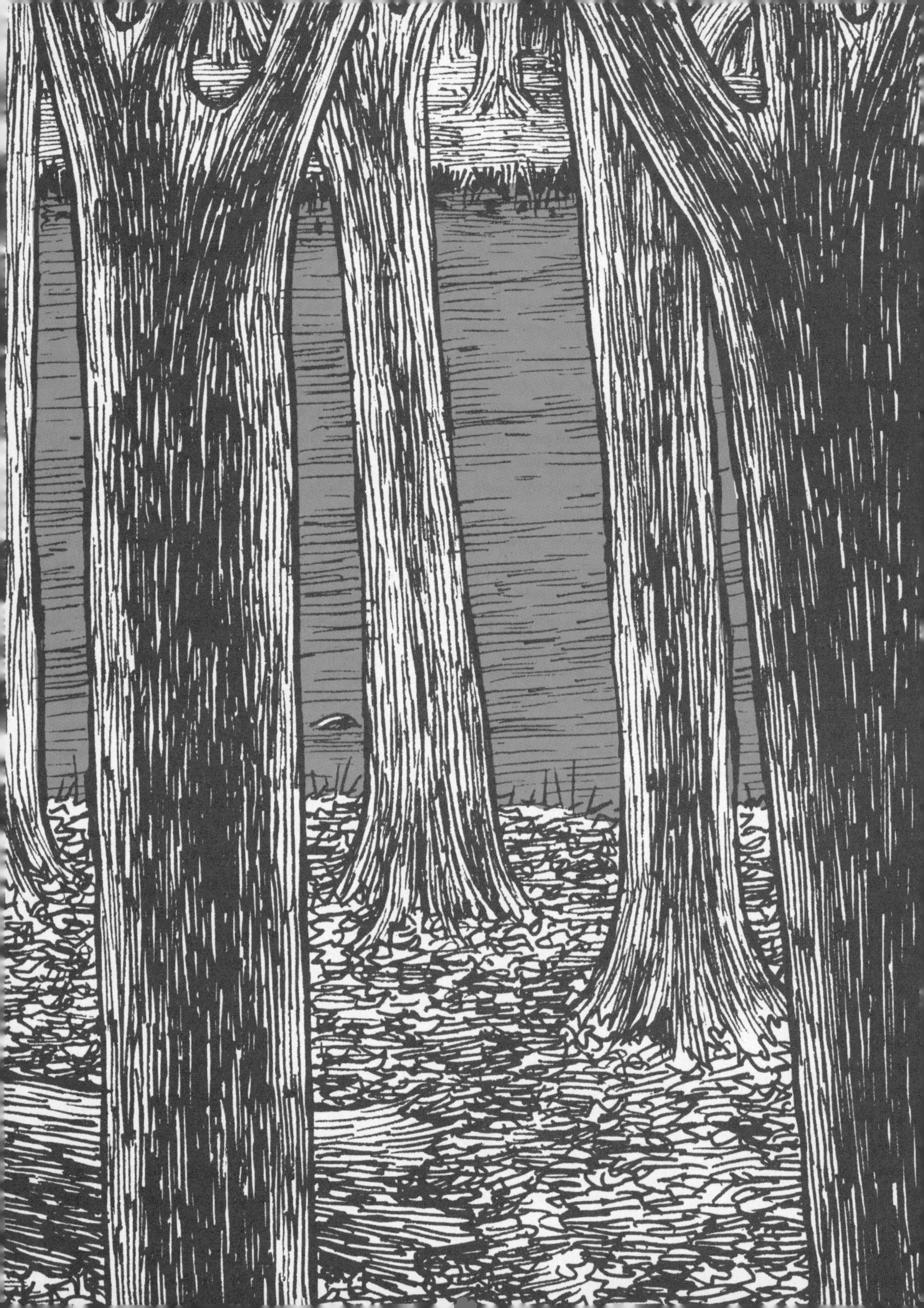

Erik De Graaf

Erik de Graaf was born in 1961 in Vlaardingen, the Nether-
lands. For the past twenty years he has worked as a graphic
designer and, although he has drawn his entire life, he only
started drawing comics two years ago when he was over 40.
Since then he has completed several short stories which have
been published in three Dutch editions by Oog + Blik, the
Holland-based publisher of R. Crumb, Chris Ware, and Joost
Swarte. One of the stories from the first collection is pre-
sented in English on the following pages.

He still lives in Vlaardingen, together with his partner, their
daughter, two cats, a rabbit and some fish.

Game

A NICE DAY IN SPRING. WE WERE THE ONLY PASSENGERS LEFT ON THE BUS

CAN YOU SEE THEM ALREADY?

NO, NOT YET.

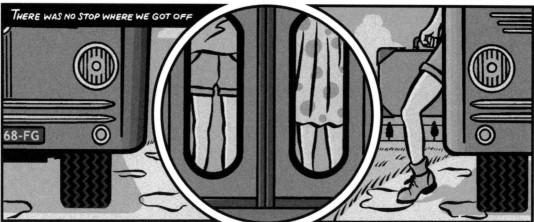

THERE WAS NO STOP WHERE WE GOT OFF

68-FG

BUT THE BUS DRIVER KNEW...

WHERE WE WERE GOING

TRANSLATED BY ROLIN VAN DE PAVERT   HAND-LETTERED BY DIRK REHM

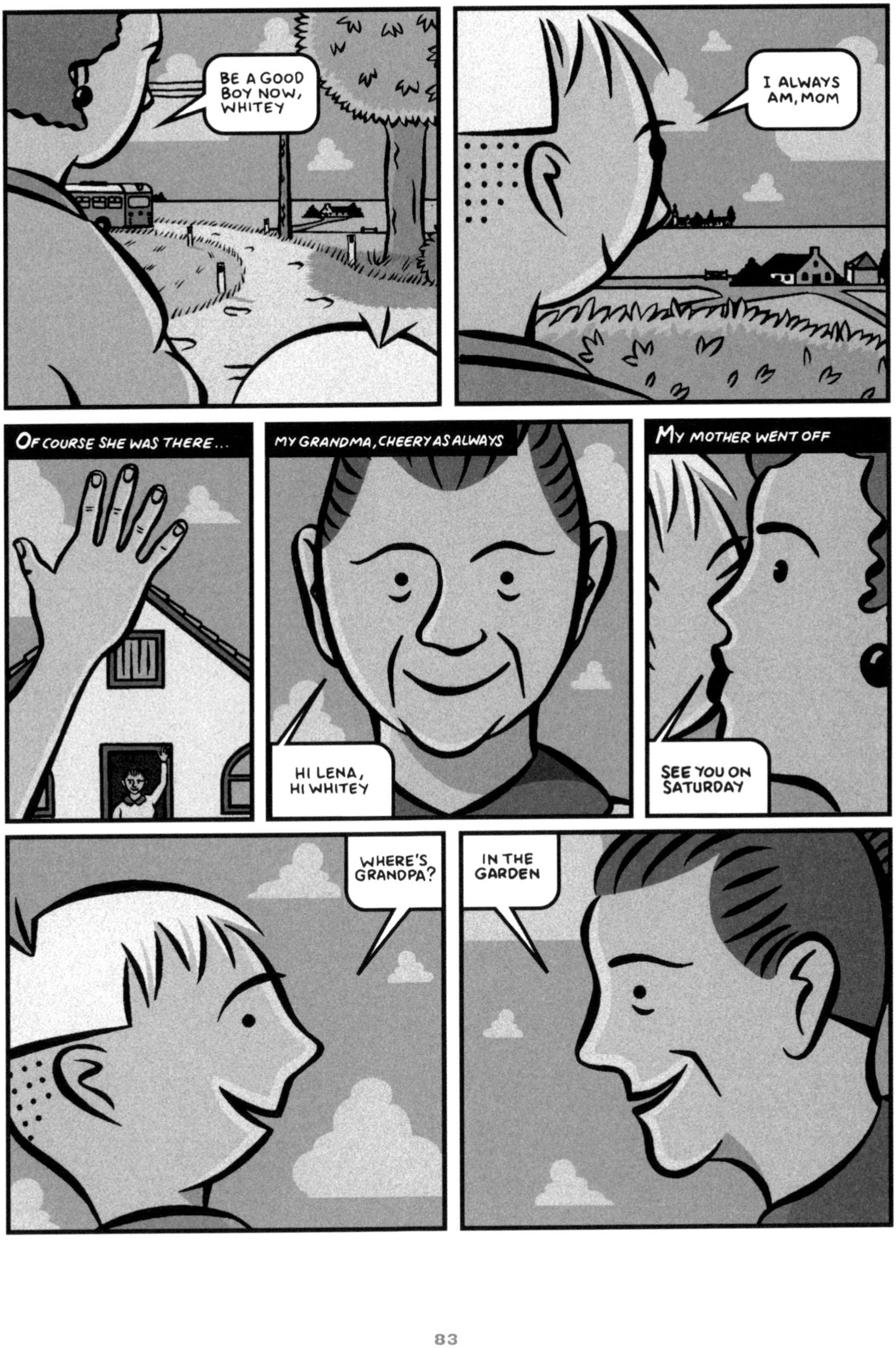
BE A GOOD BOY NOW, WHITEY
I ALWAYS AM, MOM
OF COURSE SHE WAS THERE...
MY GRANDMA, CHEERY AS ALWAYS
HI LENA, HI WHITEY
MY MOTHER WENT OFF
SEE YOU ON SATURDAY
WHERE'S GRANDPA?
IN THE GARDEN

COUGH, COUGH, COUGH...

MY GRANDDAD HAD REALLY BAD LUNGS

COUGH, COUGH, COUGH...

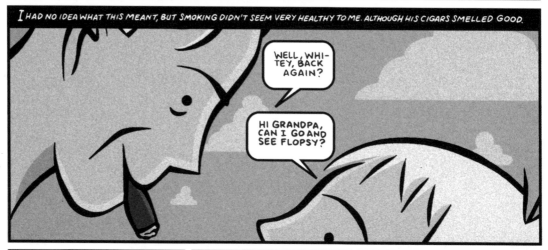

I HAD NO IDEA WHAT THIS MEANT, BUT SMOKING DIDN'T SEEM VERY HEALTHY TO ME. ALTHOUGH HIS CIGARS SMELLED GOOD.

WELL, WHI-TEY, BACK AGAIN?

HI GRANDPA, CAN I GO AND SEE FLOPSY?

FLOPSY WAS MY PET RABBIT

HE COULDN'T WALK, BECAUSE...

HI FLOPSY

HIS HIND LEGS WERE PARALYSED

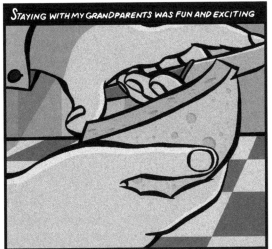

STAYING WITH MY GRANDPARENTS WAS FUN AND EXCITING

THICK SLICES OF CHEESE, LOTS OF TELEVISION...

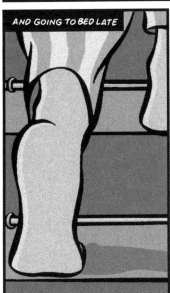

AND GOING TO BED LATE

THE FIRST NIGHT...

I OFTEN COULDN'T GET TO SLEEP

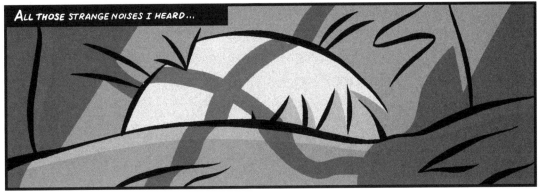

ALL THOSE STRANGE NOISES I HEARD...

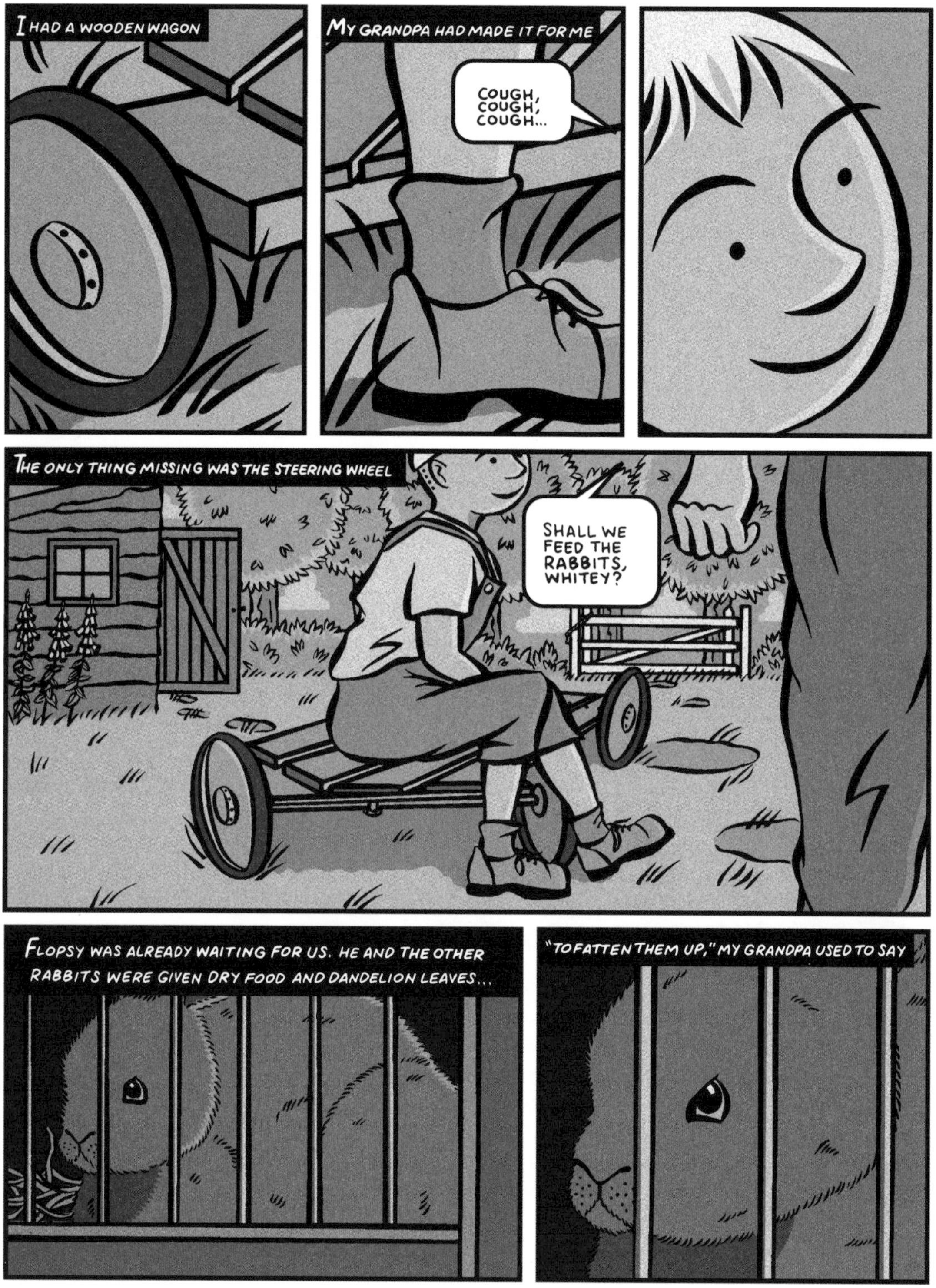
I HAD A WOODEN WAGON
MY GRANDPA HAD MADE IT FOR ME
COUGH, COUGH, COUGH...
THE ONLY THING MISSING WAS THE STEERING WHEEL
SHALL WE FEED THE RABBITS, WHITEY?
FLOPSY WAS ALREADY WAITING FOR US. HE AND THE OTHER RABBITS WERE GIVEN DRY FOOD AND DANDELION LEAVES...
"TO FATTEN THEM UP," MY GRANDPA USED TO SAY

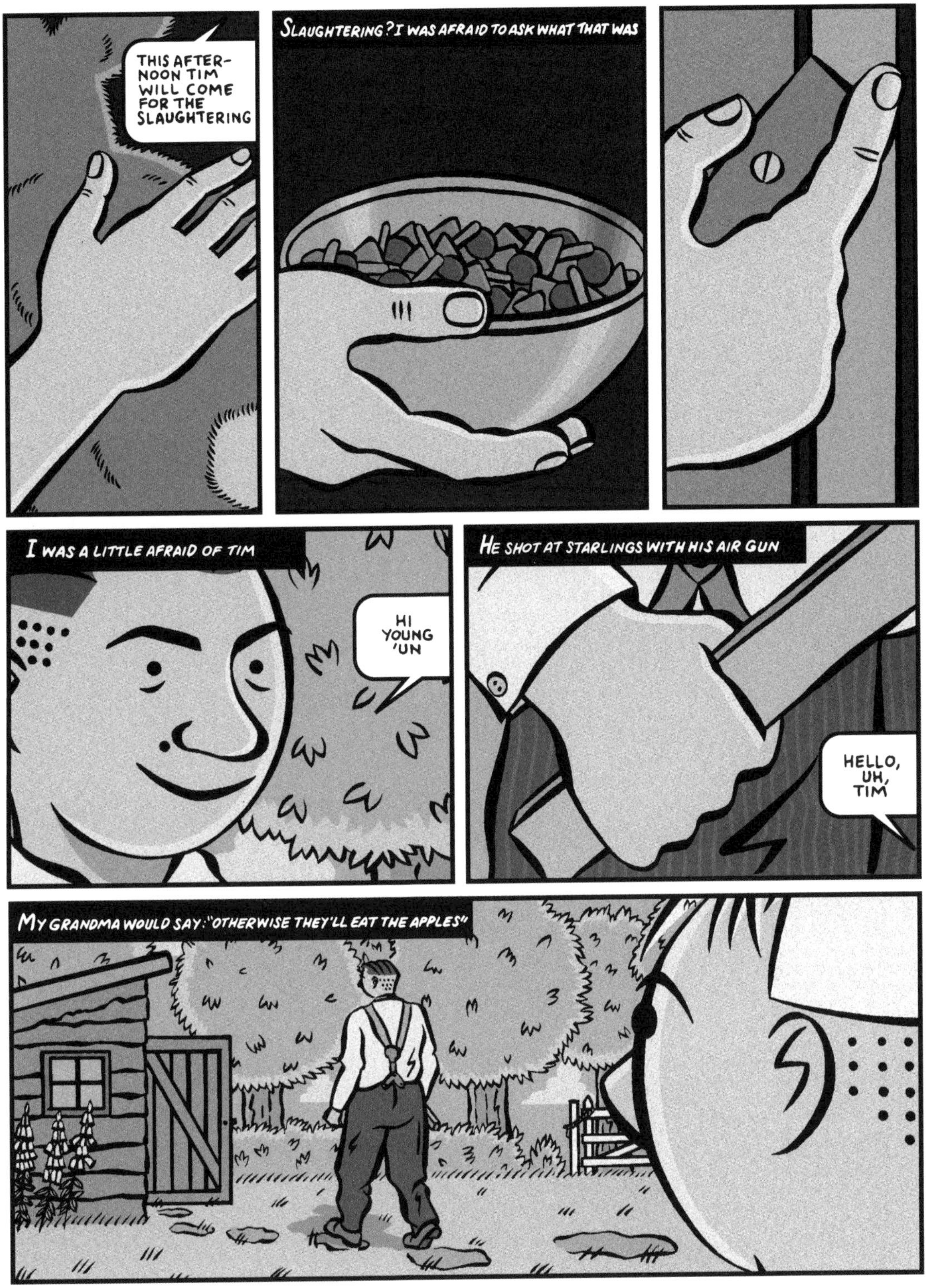
THIS AFTERNOON TIM WILL COME FOR THE SLAUGHTERING
SLAUGHTERING? I WAS AFRAID TO ASK WHAT THAT WAS
I WAS A LITTLE AFRAID OF TIM
HI YOUNG 'UN
HE SHOT AT STARLINGS WITH HIS AIR GUN
HELLO, UH, TIM
MY GRANDMA WOULD SAY: "OTHERWISE THEY'LL EAT THE APPLES"

I WAS INTRIGUED BY HIS PIMPLE

IT MADE TIM EVEN MORE TERRIFYING

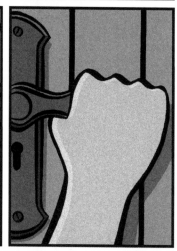

ONCE AGAIN I COULDN'T GET TO SLEEP THAT NIGHT.

I KEPT SEEING TIM'S PIMPLE. IT GOT BIGGER AND BIGGER

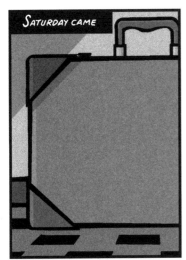

SATURDAY CAME

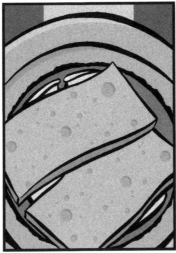

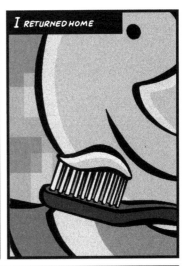

I RETURNED HOME

MY FATHER PICKED ME UP

'BYE GRANDPA

'BYE GRANDMA

COME ALONG, BOY

GRANDPA AND GRANDMA WAVED GOODBYE

27-54-JV

AND I LOOKED FOR A GLIMPSE OF TIM

54-JV

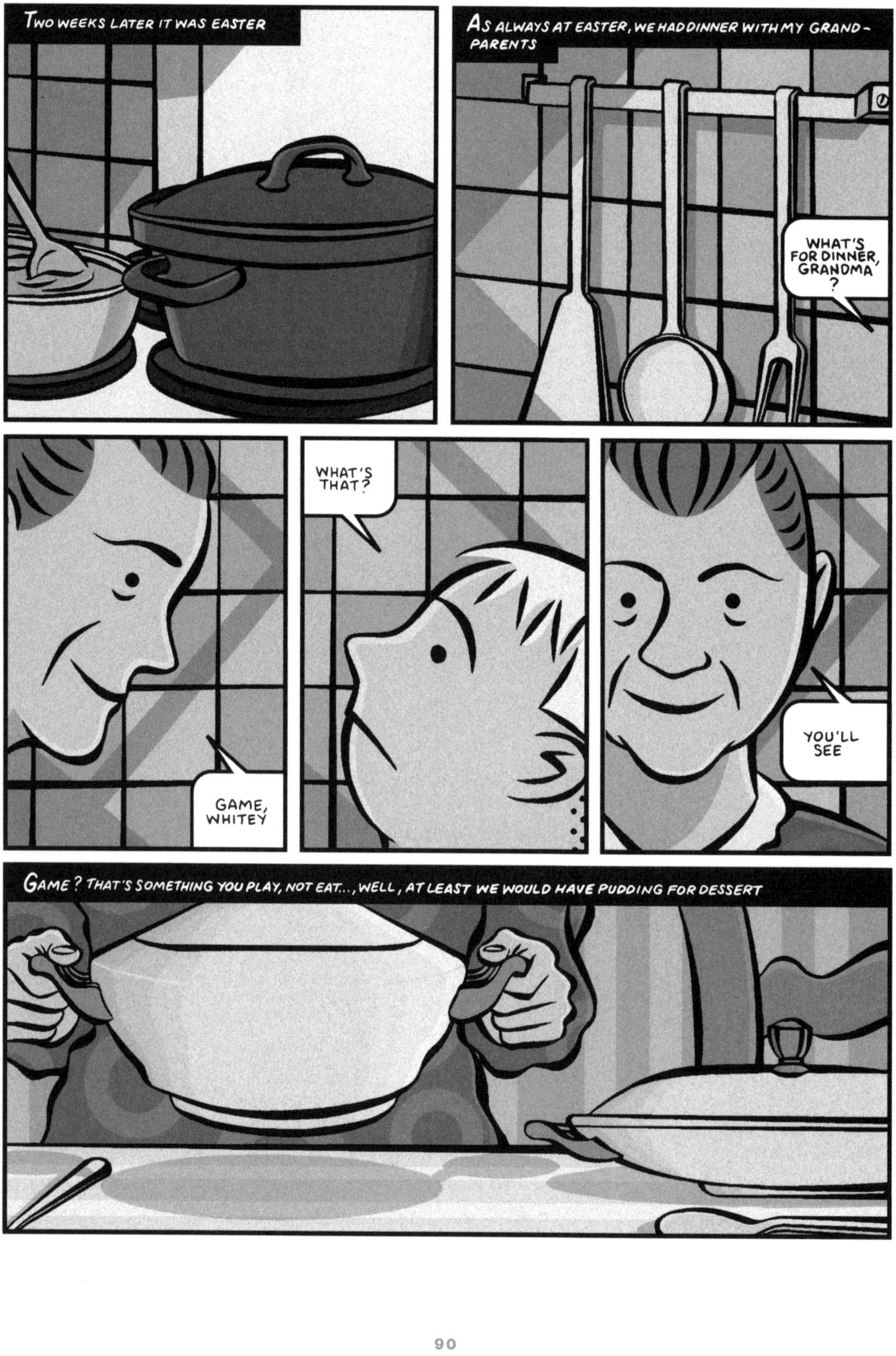
Two weeks later it was Easter
As always at Easter, we had dinner with my grand-parents
WHAT'S FOR DINNER, GRANDMA?
GAME, WHITEY
WHAT'S THAT?
YOU'LL SEE
Game? That's something you play, not eat..., well, at least we would have pudding for dessert

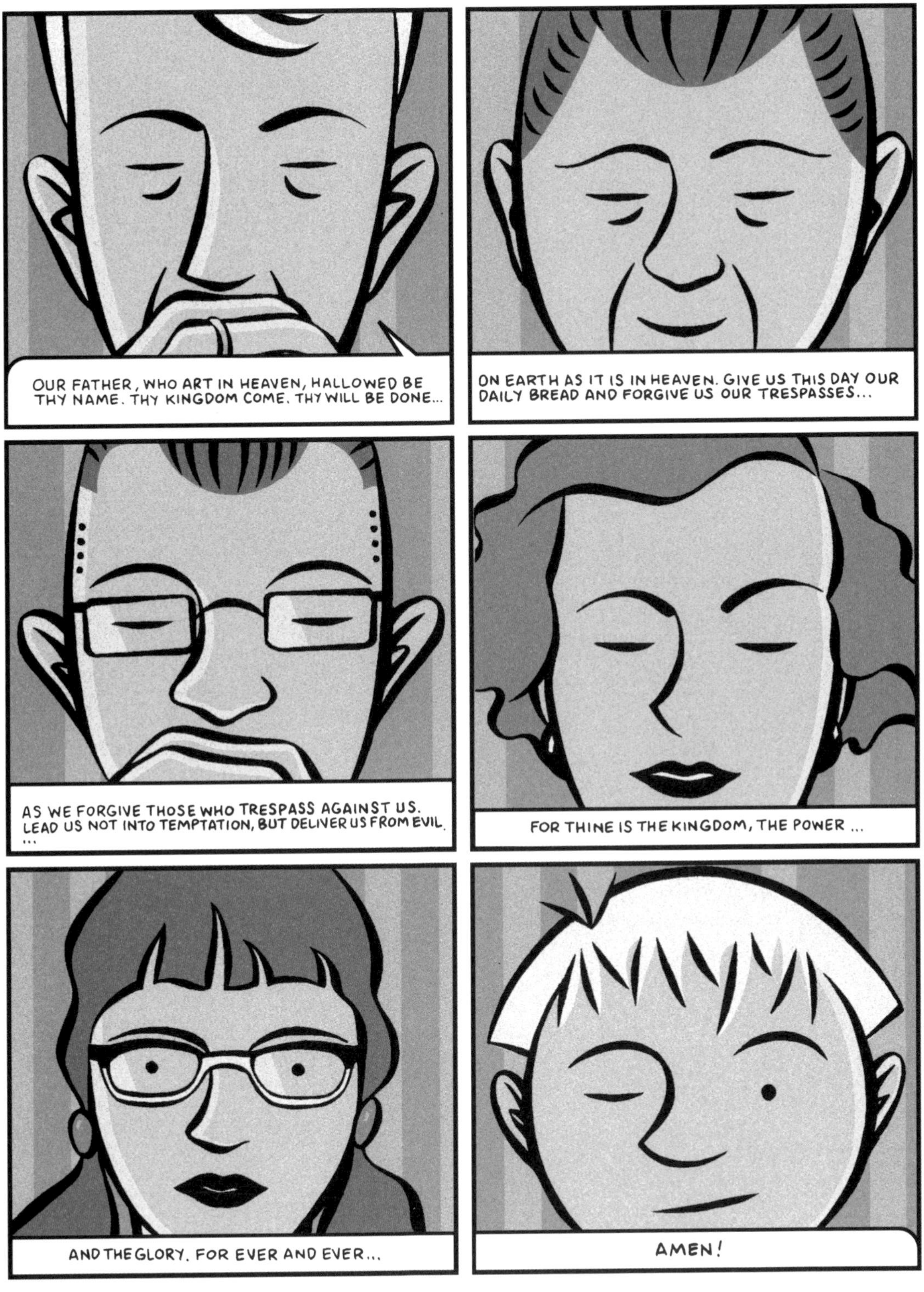
OUR FATHER, WHO ART IN HEAVEN, HALLOWED BE THY NAME. THY KINGDOM COME. THY WILL BE DONE...
ON EARTH AS IT IS IN HEAVEN. GIVE US THIS DAY OUR DAILY BREAD AND FORGIVE US OUR TRESPASSES...
AS WE FORGIVE THOSE WHO TRESPASS AGAINST US. LEAD US NOT INTO TEMPTATION, BUT DELIVER US FROM EVIL. ...
FOR THINE IS THE KINGDOM, THE POWER ...
AND THE GLORY. FOR EVER AND EVER...
AMEN!

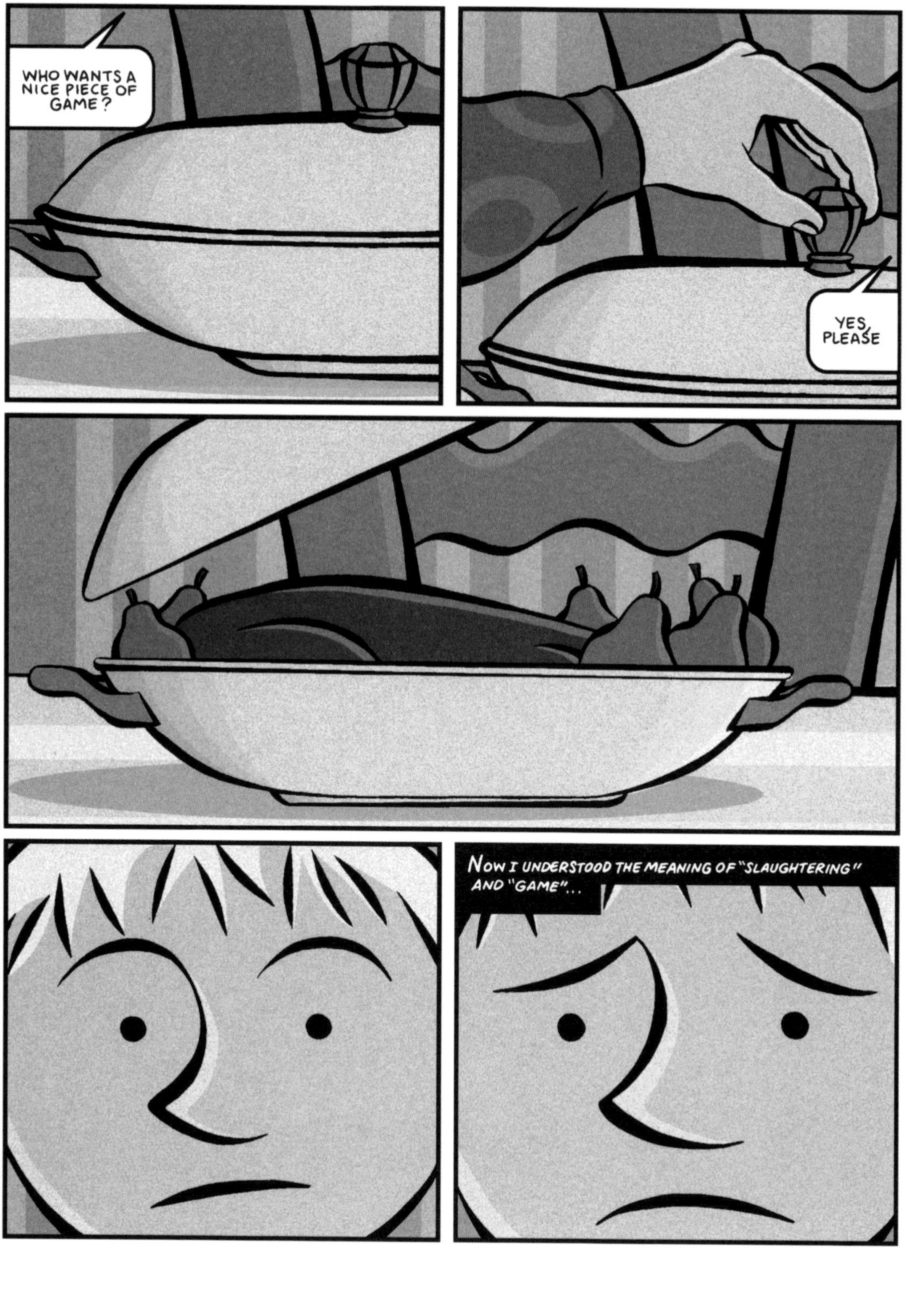
WHO WANTS A NICE PIECE OF GAME?
YES, PLEASE
NOW I UNDERSTOOD THE MEANING OF "SLAUGHTERING" AND "GAME"...

GAGGING, I RAN OUTSIDE...

AFRAID OF WHAT I MIGHT FIND

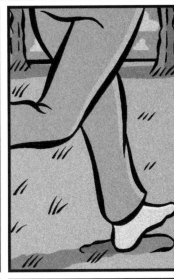

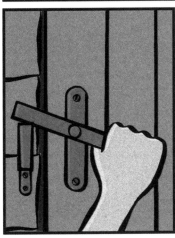

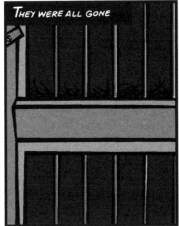

THEY WERE ALL GONE

YOU MURDERERS!

Flopsy too...

I was sure Tim and his mother were having game for dinner, too

That horrible Tim...

Let's go find him

I'll search the orchard

I'll have a look in the barn

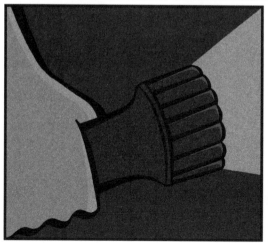

I think I've found him...

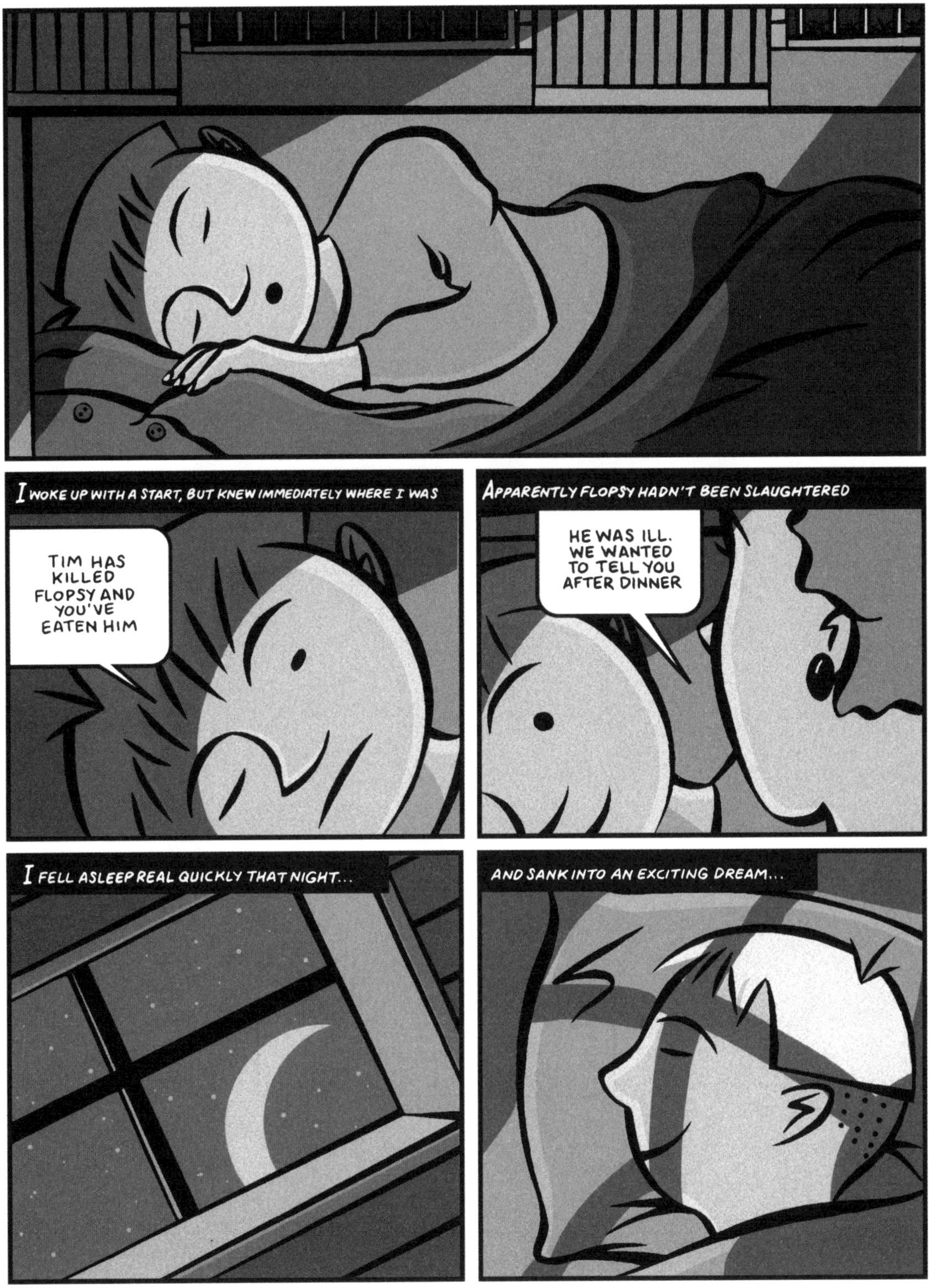
I WOKE UP WITH A START, BUT KNEW IMMEDIATELY WHERE I WAS
TIM HAS KILLED FLOPSY AND YOU'VE EATEN HIM
APPARENTLY FLOPSY HADN'T BEEN SLAUGHTERED
HE WAS ILL. WE WANTED TO TELL YOU AFTER DINNER
I FELL ASLEEP REAL QUICKLY THAT NIGHT...
AND SANK INTO AN EXCITING DREAM...

THE END